To Walk In The Way

THE COVER

In March of 1978—to highlight the spring Spiritual Life Week—Eastern Mennonite College, Harrisonburg, Virginia, became the setting for a series of studies from the Gospel of Mark. During each morning chapel period and each evening in a public meeting, Dr. Willard Swartley led the large assembly in a detailed and scholarly pilgrimage of discovery. Integrated in various ways were many of the dramatic episodes and forms which are now a part of this volume.

Urie A. Bender, author of these dramatic interpretations, was on campus throughout the rehearsal and production period, serving as consultant.

Barbara Graber, member of the first cast and production at Estes Park, Colorado, directed a cast of sixteen students in the twice-daily enactments as well as in two complete evening dramatic performances presented without the Bible study component. In the cover photo, J. David Lehman and Rachel Pellman, as disciples, narrate a scene from the miraculous feeding of the multitudes.

Cover photo by Jim Bishop, courtesy of Eastern Mennonite College.

To Walk In The Way

Dramatic interpretations from the Gospel of Mark with major credits to Johanan Marcus

Urie A. Bender

Introduction by Willard M. Swartley

For the Son of Man himself
has not come to be served
but to serve, and to give
his life to set many
others free.

*Mark 10:36,
Phillips.*

HERALD PRESS
Kitchener, Ontario
Scottdale, Pennsylvania
1979

Canadian Cataloguing in Publication Data

Bender, Urie A., 1925-
   To walk in the way

ISBN 0-8361-1884-7

1. Jesus Christ - Drama.   I. Title.

PS3552.E538T6   812'.5'4   C79-094124-4

CREDITS: A number of versions of Scripture have been used throughout this book, notably: the King James Version, the Revised Standard Version, The New Testament in Modern English (Phillips), The New English Bible, and The New International Bible. In addition, various combinations of versions are used, as well as loose paraphrases of brief portions.

TO WALK IN THE WAY
Copyright © 1979 by Urie A. Bender
Published by Herald Press, Kitchener, Ont. N2G 4M5
   Released simultaneously in the United States by
   Herald Press, Scottdale, Pa. 15683
Library of Congress Catalog Card Number: 79-83511
International Standard Book Number: 0-8361-1884-7
Printed in the United States of America
Design: Alice B. Shetler

15 14 13 12 11 10 9 8 7 6 5 4 3 2 1

To
Loretta Yoder,
whose warm encouragement, supportive skill, and
professional partnership have contributed so much
to my forays into the field of dramatic writing.

CONTENTS

Introduction by Willard M. Swartley — 9

Author's Preface — 13

How to Use *Mark: The Way for All Nations* — 21

Performance Rights Policy — 22

Production Notes — 23

PROLOGUE—There Is a Way *(Choric)* — 29

PART I—Who Is This Man?

  *Mark Introduces Jesus — 35

    Meet the Author *(Monologue)* — 36

    Jesus Appears *(Choric/Audio Vignette)* — 40

    Just Like That *(Choric)* — 45

  *Early Conflict—Jesus and the Pharisees — 49

    Healing of the Paralytic *(Vignette)* — 50

    Man with the Withered Hand *(Choric)* — 59

  *Secrets Are for Telling — 63

    Hidden Seed—Certain Harvest *(Choric/Narration)* — 64

  *Hints of Identity — 71

    Introduction *(Narration, Choric, and Music)* — 72

    The Wind and the Waves Obey *(Monologue)* — 77

    Peace, Be Still *(Choric and Music)* — 80

    I Was There *(Monologue)* — 81

    Who Is This Man?—Preamble *(Choric)* — 85

    The Gadarene Set Free *(Monologue)* — 87

    No Bondage Now—I'm Free *(Monologue)* — 91

    No Final Prison Here *(Monologue)* — 95

    Who Is This Man? *(Choric)* — 99

  *Declaration and Unveiling — 103

    Why Is the Mystery Locked Away? *(Choric)* — 104

Bread and Blindness *(Narration)* — 107
Willing to Eat the Crumbs *(Choric, Pantomime, and
    Simultaneous Audio Vignette)* — 113
Men as Trees Walking *(Choric)* — 119
Everything Sharp and Clear *(Pantomime)* — 129
Then Will . . . Eyes . . . Be Opened *(Narration)* — 130
We Have Seen His Power *(Choric)* — 131

PART II—The Kingdom Way
  *The Greatest Is Servant of All — 135
    A New Kingdom *(Choric)* — 136
    Jesters Tell the Truth *(Choric/Vignette)* — 150
    To Serve Is the Only Way *(Choric)* — 157
  *To Choose or Not to Choose the Way — 161
    A Hard Choice *(Choric)* — 162
    It Was a Sad Hour *(Monologue)* — 163

PART III—The Temple for All Nations
  *Later Conflict—Jesus and the Pharisees — 169
    The Temple Cleansed *(Vignette)* — 170
    Tenants in the Vineyard *(Narration)* — 179
  *No Curtain Now — 183
    Rent in Twain *(Choric)* — 184
    It Was a Bad Day *(Monologue)* — 187
  *Finale—The Servant Died on the
        Way to Exaltation — 191
    Marcus *(Monologue)* — 192
    After the Cross *(Narration)* — 194
    Whose Way Leads Through a Tomb *(Choric)* — 195
    There Is a Way—to Exaltation *(Choric)* — 198

EPILOGUE — 203
LITANY OF CONFESSION — 211
Author — 223

Note: All starred lines represent groupings of material which relate to the Bible study companion volume. (See How to Use *Mark: The Way for All Nations*, page 21.)

INTRODUCTION

During the last decade a new trend has emerged in the field of biblical scholarship. This trend—headlined by storytelling, structuralist hermeneutic, liberation hermeneutic, and the use of a psychoanalytic bridge between Scripture and ourselves—points to the dual concern for Scripture to speak to us on its own terms as well as to address us with an answer for our needs today.

It may be the surfacing of this basic universal need which explains the phenomenal public response to a variety of new media which today are communicating the biblical message. For example, the *Wall Street Journal* of July 7, 1978, reported that " 'St. Mark' is now one of the hottest tickets in the commercial West End theatres" in London. On a bare stage stand three wooden chairs and a wooden table on which sets a pitcher of water and a glass. The performance consists of a one-man recitation of Mark's Gospel, word for word from the King James Version by Britain's well-known actor, Alec McCowen.

In September 1978, McCowen began a three-month tour of performances in the United States. *Time* magazine (September 18, 1978) reported on the unique dynamics of McCowen's performance—a recitation that *tells* the story, with effects depending on the action of the story itself and McCowen's masterful use of his voice.

The approach proposed by Walter Wink in *The Bible in Human Transformation* emphasizes the relevance of the biblical message. It seeks to build a bridge between the fruits of biblical scholarship and our need to experience the Scripture as a transforming source of power. The rising number of small Bible study groups throughout circles of Christian believers and seekers witnesses also to a new openness toward biblical knowledge and guidance.

Urie Bender's volume of dramatic interpretations, *To Walk in the Way,* fits naturally into the stream of endeavor which beckons the multitude to hear afresh the biblical message. Integrally related to its companion volume, *Mark: The Way for All Nations,* the drama inherent in Bender's book represents one kind of pioneering contribution in the use of old forms to release and communicate the drama inherent in the biblical message—especially to those who are willing to hear the Scriptures in a new dialect by way of a medium that elicits holistic response—through thought, feeling, attitude, and action.

The origin of these dramatic interpretations from Mark's Gospel has its own unique history, narrated by both Bender in the Preface that follows and by myself in the Preface to the companion volume, *Mark: The Way for All Nations.* Quite significantly, the dramatic resources of this volume did not originate simply from one person's desire to write drama on the Bible. The history of the genesis of this work tells of communal birth and growth.

One aspect of this communal venture consisted of Bender's serious effort to acquire scholarly, exegetical knowledge of Mark's Gospel. Bender did not approach his task by imposing his own notions upon the text; he spent much time immersing himself not only in the Gospel, but in several scholarly interpretations as well.

As Bender indicates in his Preface, he seeks "to be exegetically correct and at the same time to release the dramatic impact of Mark's view of Jesus Christ." In this attempt Bender has done well—at the cost of experiencing the pain of pruning off branches extending into other biblical themes laden with delicious dramatic fruit but which, nonetheless, blunt and dilute the distinctive emphasis of Mark.

Bender's contribution is not biblical drama only for the sake of drama; it is dramatic interpretation which grows naturally out of the text and thus remains fully in the service of the biblical text. From my point of view, because the exegetical task has informed these dramatic interpretations, they are authentic and powerful. Accordingly, use of this material in its separate parts in conjunction with study of the corresponding chapters in *Mark: The Way for All Nations* increases the effectiveness of both these dramatic interpretations and the Bible studies. Especially for those who have studied the entire Gospel, the production and experience of seeing/hearing the full drama has the potential of becoming an event of intense spiritual significance.

With deep gratitude for Bender's creative gift to biblical interpretation, I anticipate wide use of *To Walk in the Way*—for the cause of the kingdom of God.

Canadian Thanksgiving Day
October 9, 1978

Willard M. Swartley
Associated Mennonite
    Biblical Seminaries
Elkhart, Indiana

AUTHOR'S PREFACE

As a writer, Mark excels. His account of Jesus' life and teachings moves superbly from a beginning of stark impact to an ending with singular power.

The content of his message about the Christ is shaped carefully through varied literary techniques: a thoughtful selection of material, sparse but essential detail, straightforward language, subtle nuances inherent in form and sequence, conflict, suspense, masterful use of character and incident to build toward climax. His characters are painted with spare, incisive strokes. His reporting—the words spoken by Jesus, the questing of his disciples, the reactions of family, of the multitudes, of the religious leaders—reflects the work of an honest craftsman who, through the record he has left, also outlines his personal search as well as his certain conclusions.

All this, and more, became clear to me when I—another writer—began to peruse Mark's Gospel in preparation for a brief dramatic writing assignment in connection with Bible study periods at Mennonite General Assembly, Estes Park, Colorado, in June of 1977. This early perusal grew into lengthy research, then into a captivating commitment to discover ways past the clichés which have numbed many readers of the New Testament message. As never before, I became aware of the high drama inherent in Jesus' incarnation of kingdom principles. Through Mark's eyes I began to see the powerful story he had to tell. I was gripped by a seemingly similar compulsion to show my fellows the full force of the message about another kingdom, a kingdom way of life, which the Christ taught and embodied.

What began as an invitation became then, for me, a commission I could not escape. The pages which follow appear as a result, apparently somewhat final in character as is usually true of the printed page. The astute reader, however, will perceive quickly that these dramatic interpretations signal only a beginning.

The beginning of a whole new way of reading the Scriptures. The beginning of dissatisfaction with old forms which no longer carry the impact the message deserves. The beginning of awareness that real people inhabit the Gospels: people with thoughts and feelings, with weaknesses and doubts, with aspirations and hopes; people whose impact on posterity is not reduced, but rather enhanced, by their earthiness and pervasive humanity; people rendered no less important to us by the fact that their lives are now history. Thus was my commitment formed. To this end I gave my energies. Within this vision, I was pursued by the conviction that partnership between Bible scholar, writer, and dramatic director was a viable and exciting frontier.

Specifically, credit must be given to Professor Willard Swartley for his willingness to allow scholarly work and dramatic interpretation an opportunity to merge their strengths. His grasp of this Gospel's message, his dedication to correct exegesis and the openhearted sharing of his own insights made my necessary research a joy. His warm encouragement, his patience, and his sensitivity to the creative process brightened the tedious days of writing and lightened the difficult pressures during rehearsals and production. Partnership in creation, risky and tenuous at best, became in this instance an awesome experience.

In this setting thanks is due also to Loretta Yoder, whose deep commitment to enactment as a medium of worship and whose finely tuned skills as an interpretive director brought our first productions at Estes Park to the level of excellence they enjoyed. Supporting her, of course, were cast members who offered dedication and their own perspective along with unusual energies to a script that was still in the birthing process—only half-finished at that date.

A second series of dramatic interpretations, joined with Bible study, was carried out in March of 1978 at Eastern Mennonite College during Spiritual Renewal Week. Professor Swartley led the studies in Mark; Loretta Yoder served as a consultant during auditions; and Barbara Graber (one in the first cast of seven) directed a cast of sixteen students in interpretative expression during nine study periods and two full-length dramatic renderings. Some of the segments represented repeat performances; other performances were based entirely on new material.

Obviously, a number of persons have been involved in the growth of this script. Various rehearsal and production settings have contributed working insights toward revisions. The final molding has come about almost as much by "on-stage editing" as by creation and rewriting in solitude. To strike a balance of recognition between all participating persons is difficult. At the same time, of course, it must be said that I bear full responsibility for the writing now in your hand.

Credit to these—as well as to the Gospel writer—highlights another cause for thanksgiving: the work of the Spirit of God in creative effort. As is clear, the entire script is rooted in Mark's material. His objectives helped to shape my intention. His insights illumined for me the way of the kingdom and how to walk in that way. His selections of incidents—his overall sense of story—have drawn a profile of the Christ of that way. Willard Swartley, a contemporary scholar, has been my tutor, so his interpretations are present in my views. To this I have brought my personal background, my own objectives, the flavor of my own understanding, my own creative shaping. Others have added their gifts. But through it all there has been a pervasive Presence. The Spirit of God has been at work forming diverse skills and experiences into an amalgam which, in expression and enactment, has uncovered for some of us the drama which led Mark to pen the Gospel that now bears his name.

The words *drama* and *dramatic* are difficult words—often misused, therefore often misunderstood. Contrary to a popular misconception, drama does not inhere necessarily in a particular form as such. Rather, it is uncovered by or emerges as the result of an artistic or dramatic expression. In other words, the use of a dramatic form does not guarantee drama. A play or a pantomime or a monologue may be only that, and not drama at all. On the other hand, certain content coming to life through appropriate forms and agents may, before and within a receptive audience, allow real drama to be perceived and experienced.

In some eras and places, *drama* and *dramatic* have been linked exclusively with *theater* and *stage*. Where these latter terms have suffered unsavory connotations, the use of dramatic forms in other settings has also suffered. Consequently, Christians have too frequently denied themselves insights and growth opportunities because they have not distinguished between the various uses of dramatic expression.

This manuscript assumes that dramatic forms are useful to the Christian pilgrim. In fact, it assumes that drama is generic to Christian faith. It assumes further that a dramatic moment has the ability to draw us to levels of awareness beyond those we ordinarily experience or consider possible. The Scriptures come alive in new ways—thus our understanding is enlightened. We "feel with" characters and "into" incidents which typically have become clichés—thus our emotions become engaged. Insights demand response—thus our wills are confronted. It is at this point where long-established categories are assaulted.

Drama has been identified usually as *art* with a consequent requirement that each expression reflect its own integrity—that neither content nor expressional form be prostituted by intentions external to themselves. Generally, the *Bible* has been seen as *didactic,* with that purpose overriding every other conceivable good. Further, *didactic* has been seen in the context of a narrow methodology and largely in the context of stated objective rather than surprising or unexpected result. Stated thus, the categories of *art* and *didacticism* are mutually exclusive.

This attitude of exclusivism has been nurtured by both Bible scholars and artists. Bible scholars and theologians, driven by their zeal for precise understandings, find it difficult to tolerate emotion-laden vehicles of individual or group expression which are not fully predictable. Conversely, the artist along with literary and drama critics—all committed to artistic integrity—can hardly conceive of a didactic result which has not somehow compromised either content or form.

It should be obvious that I have neither the wisdom nor the space in these several paragraphs to propose a carefully reasoned resolution of this impasse. There is no single or simple response. Only continuing dialogue may open up some new glimmers of light.

At the same time, I find myself resisting those who demand the security of their categories. Categories are often antithetical to creativity. And I question whether true creativity in any generation dare ever be fully locked in by the literary or scholarly mores of an illustrious and useful past. Indeed, to carry my reaction a step further, if the message of Mark's Gospel has any bearing on this point, one is forced to declare a willingness to see old forms broken apart by the dynamic of new life erupting again and again to meet a present need—each such eruption shaping itself into a form hitherto unfamiliar.

One can speak of fidelity to the biblical record with all the light that ancient and modern scholars can shed on the message. And one can speak of fidelity to the artistic vision—integrity in script and expression. Viewed as opposites, they are presumed to be in conflict.

Or—to take a leap beyond both—one may speak of fidelity to truth. Suspending for the moment our familiar responses, is it possible to accept a view that sees in a new light the human condition or the high drama of incarnation, the awesome experience of living by faith though still in the material context of time and space, the miracle of God's grace invading that context to bring into being a new kingdom of which we may be part?

For me, then, the tension between the didactic and the artistic becomes petty and irrelevant, falsely perpetuated by those to whom categories have become security. A commitment to truth justifies the scholar's search; it shapes the dramatic moment; it electrifies the commitment of audience and cast to each other; it forces mind and heart and will into confrontation. What follows is a matter of choice.

Seen in the light of a joint commitment to truth, artistic integrity and careful biblical scholarship become partners, neither violating the other. Each form of expression possesses its own integrity. For the hovering Spirit of God continues to bring into being those new creations which "people" our world and point unerringly to divine purpose clothed in flesh with all the resultant agony and ecstasy and conflict. That is high drama! And we could do worse than search for ways to reflect that drama on our own path toward likeness to His image—whatever forms that search may take.

The partnership between biblical scholarship and artistic integrity, referred to above, has been close to the heart of my excitement throughout the period I worked in the Gospel of Mark. Often that excitement grew into motivation, even compulsion, as new vistas appeared.

If now—to the reader and the user, to each student and each actor, to some director and some audience—is given a sense of newness in Mark's Gospel, an awareness of the dramatic force present whenever men and women open their lives to God's power and grace, a recognition that His kingdom is here and now wherever disciples follow in the way of Christ, then the mating of these disciplines will have borne fruit and the writer will have his ample reward.

Publication of this manuscript of dramatic interpretations jointly with a carefully worked out Bible study guide, in some sense, is an experiment. Separate volumes—with each keyed to the other—obviously was deliberate: a concession to those who might prefer to use one or the other exclusively. A recognition also that, placed together, the entire volume would be unwieldy. However, some part of the hope and intention of the two authors will be lost if the interlinking strengths of both forms of approach are totally ignored.

Both Professor Swartley and I feel as if we've embarked together on a unique and intriguing voyage. The attempt to work in concert—to be exegetically correct and at the same time to release the dramatic impact of Mark's view of Jesus Christ—has brought constant exhilaration, sometimes nagging apprehensions, and also rare fulfillments. Our sense of direction so far has been clear but neither of us finds any hint of compass heading beyond the horizon. For this we will need—and we do welcome—the responses of those who work with the material in local settings.

Mention has been made already of those directly involved in various stages of development of this script. But I would be remiss not to include thanks to Dottie, my wife, for her continuing support throughout a project which grew from an expected two weeks to a demanding twelve months; to Linda (Emch), our daughter, whose spirit tuned to mine continued to provide sustenance and whose typing assistance freed me for creative work; to those friends whose assurance of closeness and love and prayers brought courage when either research or writing became an intense spiritual battle; and finally to the publisher whose simultaneous acceptance and joint publication of manuscripts by two different authors brought him also into a partnership of risk. To each and to all must be inscribed this word of deep gratefulness.

No work of mine in the past has gone forth with more trepidation or with more anticipation. I pray that the first will have been unnecessary and that the latter is justified.

In the name of Jesus,
Urie A. Bender
August 31, 1978

How to Use
MARK: THE WAY FOR ALL NATIONS
With This Book

Willard Swartley's book, *Mark: The Way for All Nations,* can provide an enriching backdrop for these dramatic interpretations. None of the dramatic interpretations in this script require introductory or parallel Bible study sessions. However, the Bible study materials in Swartley's companion volume (Herald Press, 1979) do provide valuable process and insights crucial to a fuller understanding of Mark's message.

To simplify the integration of study and dramatic expression wherever this is desired, the following outline is offered:

Bender's *To Walk in the Way*	Swartley's *Mark: The Way for All Nations*
There Is a Way	Throughout
Mark Introduces Jesus	Chapter 1
Early Conflict—Jesus and the Pharisees	Chapter 2
Secrets Are for Telling	Chapter 3
Hints of Identity	Chapters 4, 5
Declaration and Unveiling	Chapter 6
The Greatest Is Servant of All	Chapter 7
To Choose or Not to Choose the Way	Chapter 8
Later Conflict—Jesus and the Pharisees	Chapter 9
No Curtain Now	Chapter 10
Finale—The Servant Died on the Way to Exaltation	Chapter 11

PERFORMANCE RIGHTS POLICY

The author and publisher are anxious to encourage the widest possible use of dramatic material in *To Walk in the Way*. Accordingly, no written permission is required and no performance royalties are charged for any portion of this book read or performed in worship services, Sunday school classes, or other similar regular congregational meetings.

This policy is based on the assumption that participants are working from purchased copies of the book. No part of this book may be reproduced in any form without written permission from the publisher.

When these materials are used in more formal dramatic performances where admission is charged or a donation is requested, written permission from the publisher is required as well as payment of the following performance royalty:

> up to 50 pages   —$15.00
> over 50 pages   —$25.00
> *or* 10% of gross (whichever is larger)

The above scale applies to performances produced by churches, educational organizations, and other non-professional groups. Theatre troupes, regular drama groups, and schools or universities with drama departments are considered professional. Here percentage of gross will normally apply unless unusual circumstances warrant special arrangements. All unauthorized uses for public performance are considered to be infringements of literary property rights.

Address your requests to Permissions Department, Herald Press, 616 Walnut Avenue, Scottdale, Pa 15683.

PRODUCTION NOTES

In recognition of the fact that some who read these pages may be interested in performance possibilities, I am sharing here some of my notes accumulated during the productions referred to. Although sketchy, they are offered with the hope that they will assist particularly those who have had less experience in dramatic productions.

Structure—These dramatic interpretations from Mark reflect a dual focus: segments in various forms, as well as a sequential whole. Except for those materials whose function is obviously transitional, any segment can stand alone dramatically, thus allowing integration as a single unit for a Bible study period, a Sunday school class, or a worship service. Most groups will likely find this pattern to be most feasible.

More demanding is the use of this script as a continuous whole. By design it follows the general plan of Mark's Gospel with relationship and sequence of segments fitted carefully into an overall pattern. Transitions are provided to make a continuous production easier. Additionally, selected Scripture passages may be used. The use of Mark as Narrator at certain points enhances the possibility of a full production using the entire script—or most of it.

However, a word of caution may be in order. Although a complete and continuous production is possible, it probably should not be attempted unless all involved have faced realistically the demands on time and energy that essential rehearsals and the production itself require. Sheer length is perhaps the most formidable factor.

Accordingly, another alternative should be mentioned. A creative director, working alone or with a worship leader or Bible teacher, could "serve Mark *a la carte,*" as it were, with thoughtful selections of material carefully arranged into a cohesive whole which would relate specifically to some theme being emphasized within a local congregational setting. Of course, the selection of segments or any major rearrangement of materials carries with it a serious responsibility not to distort the Markan emphases. Theological falsehoods may easily be perpetrated unless scrupulous attention is given to the intent of the Gospel writer.

Style of Presentation—The writer's intention for use has been enactment rather than in the form of reader's theater. A range of opportunities to test this idea, since the material was first written, confirms the original intention. Enactment, including memorization, makes possible a much fuller and more meaningful experience for all the participants—cast and audience. Of course, any form of use can be considered legitimate, including non-presentational: general reading, meditation, or private study.

Directorial Suggestions—To those readers with professional training and experience, some of the stage directions or hints to director and cast will seem redundant or limiting. Those with less exposure to the world of dramatic interpretation may find themselves wishing for more explicit guidance. To each I apologize for this attempt at "middle ground," believing that our common purposes will help our understanding of that which, at one and the same time, appears both gratuitous and inadequate or sketchy.

Of course, both the novice and the experienced dramatist will know that there is no substitute for careful study of the script. Conscientious attention to intent and expression will then allow a kind of freedom within which the original creative vision may even be enlarged.

Technical Support Elements—Throughout will be found

suggestive references to costume, lighting, sound, and other technical matters. These are included to offer possible guidance to those who may wish to test their skills in a more sophisticated production. However, nothing in these suggestions should be construed as limiting the whole or any segment to production in a facility where technical systems are up-to-date or where skills in costuming, set design, lighting, or sound are easily available. The intent, from the outset, has been to provide material which will "play" anywhere, in whole or in part, with or without elaborate technical support.

Choric Segments—The term *choric* as used here refers to a speaking chorus intended to function as a unit or with different combinations of voices. As a form which utilizes both sound and movement it allows almost infinite variations. Visual impact joined to volume, cadence, nonverbal sound, contrast, and balance can create an unforgettable setting within which communication assumes new dimensions.

The director may cast a probable minimum of four persons—using the familiar four-part structure for harmony as his base. Multiples may be added, although it should be noted that above sixteen or twenty persons, the group will be saved from becoming unwieldy and imprecise only if director and choric members are skilled in this form—through previous experience or dedication to a realistic rehearsal schedule. Careful selection of a strong but malleable group shaped by a director with clear objectives will bring into being an instrument of rare beauty and power.

Enactment of the Jesus Role—The author has made a serious effort to avoid offending persons or groups whose convictions and conscience would be violated by a Jesus-figure role played continuously by one person. Consequently, much of the development takes place from a viewpoint which renders this unnecessary. Where a Jesus voice is indicated, there are alternate methods of handling the scene: a voice cluster of three or four persons, male and female voices al-

ternating, or several persons taking turns. Conversely, all se-
quences marked *AUDIO* may also be done live offstage or, in
select settings, performed onstage with discreet and careful
lighting.

Choreographed Movement—Although not essential to
the understanding, carefully designed movements may well
add considerable beauty, meaning, and impact to the
presentation of choric segments. Movements need not be
complex but should affirm and support the message as well as
the mood. Since many religious audiences, heretofore, have
been denied or have denied themselves enjoyment of this gift
from God, movements should be discreetly restrained, appropriate, and without suggestiveness. Naturally, the extent of
the choreographic skills available will help to give final shape
to essential blocking and movement patterns.

PROLOGUE

There Is a Way

CHORIC

There is a way . . .
        marked across the geography of time
        . . . a torturous way
        . . . a joyful way
                        at times
                dropping into the valleys of everyday
                mortality;
                        at the same time
                transcending body and place,
                and wending
                a heady path
                past the peaks of eternal reality
glistening
            (in)
evening's promise
            (of)
a new day
                                . . . a way
which now and then
            is clearly seen
            or suddenly hid from view
now sharply shaped
each rocky detail
            and
twisting form
stark—

                    then (and most often)
                    both feet and path
                    lost in an earthy haze
so that each step—
          made firmly
          —must be made
in faith.
. . . a way
          —marked by one
          who has walked it
          in
          both directions—
          marked by one

                              who
                    being in the form of God
                    did not count equality with God
                              a thing
                              to be grasped (but)
                    stripped himself of all privilege

                    consented
                              to become
servant

                              and be born
mortal man

                              stripped
                              servant
                              mortal

                    (what further humbling
                    could grace command?)

this one
walked
the way to death . . .

      . . . the servant died
      on the way
      to exaltation

the servant died
on the way
to exaltation

Part 1
WHO IS THIS MAN?

MARK INTRODUCES JESUS

Meet the Author
Monologue

*(LIGHTS FADE IN SLOWLY during the
first lines.)*

MARCUS

Death was a way of life—so to speak—for the followers of
Jesus. Especially was this true in the latter days of Nero Clau-
dius Caesar, Emperor at Rome. He was a brutal man who . . .

*(PAUSE as Marcus becomes aware of the
audience.)*

. . . my pardon, I beg you. My name is Marcus, Johanan
Marcus. Some of you may know my writings; they bear my
name, though much I wrote came from the lips of my father
in the faith.

Simon Peter was kinsman to my mother. After my father
died, it was he who came each year to see if there was ought
he could do to help. It was he who first taught me the way of
Christ. And he later whom I served—at the last in Rome
where he, imprisoned, still preached that Jesus was indeed the
Christ.

Those were heavy days. The burning of Rome was laid at the
feet of the Christ-followers. Many were slaughtered—some in

the arena, torn apart by hungry beasts, 'tis said, while raucous cheers rent the air. Others, clad in clothing dipped in wax and pitch bound high upon crude poles along the Appian Way, were set to flame by torch while their burning lit the upturned jeering faces of the crowd below.

That I saw with these eyes of mine one night wrapped tight in my cloak and cowl against the searching gaze. That, I have not forgotten.

As I said, Peter was in prison; Paul also. I ministered to both with a strange freedom. It was well known to those who held the keys at each dungeon in the north wall that I also named the name of Christ. But no hand was laid upon me to stay my journeys—first to the one, and then to the other—bringing news and comfort and betimes some extra food to each alone in their dank cells.

I remember Peter speaking of the day when he, at his request, was led forth in chains to an outer courtyard, to see the sun again. A cohort of Caesar's knights was there, kept close awaiting his pleasure at some of his games. Restless they were. Peter asked to speak to them and was given leave.

From a low wall he held forth of Jesus from Nazareth and his new way. Silent they sat as he expounded the Scriptures and told them that Jesus in the flesh was indeed a word from the highest God, for Gentile as well as Jew. But in the end they set up a clamor crying, "Where is this new way writ? How can we know more?"

With that the jailer suddenly seemed to fear and with their questions still echoing loud, he gave an order and the guards rough-pushed Peter into a corridor, out of sight, and led him back to his dungeon where, the morning after, he told with joy of the witness he had made.

But his heart, he said, was also afraid. These were Caesar's knights—one of three cohorts kept always on the ready to guard him at the games or in his summer palace. If his bold words should reach the ears of Nero . . .

. . . I can see yet his gaze upon me as his eyes finished the sentence.

And I can hear yet the quiet urgency in his voice: "You must gather all your scrolls, the fragments we have used. What you have written; what I have spoken. All of them. No other one can frame them together as you. It is time."

The words which now you read I wrote then.

I did as he bade me—laid out the parchments with my hasty scrawls; those also I penned with care to read in assembly. All of them—reminders, accounts of healing at the hand of Jesus, some words he spoke (each time Peter remembered out loud, I set them down), questions, notes of my own searching struggle to know who this man was.

My early writings were all of doubt and puzzle. Faith did not come easy to me. For many months I was held in thrall by questions which were larger than the answers. But there came a time when I stepped also, willingly, in his way—and have until this day.

I was born into wealth. Although my father, until he died, required me to labor, we never knew want. Nor later, with the mother. There was the large garden of olive trees on the side of the mount, across the brook Cedron. We called it Gethsemane—the place from which I fled naked, to escape the mob when they took Jesus. We had a press also, for the ripe olives—not only our own; in the season we pressed for the others also—those on the west slope.

That press was the cause of my first sight of Jesus from Nazareth. But more of that later, perhaps.

Thus that long search came to fruit and I—in the weeks which followed Peter's death—labored with holy zeal to make a clear record of what I knew to be the truth. Nor did I shrink to write large the question that thrust itself upon my heart those many months: who is this man?

For only then could my words be true.

I remember the day Simon Peter told my mother and me of the Jordan, of John called the Baptist who was baptizing all who were wont to follow his teaching of a mighty prophet to come.

(LIGHTS—SLOW FADE OUT on Mark.)

Jesus Appears

(LIGHTS UP on Choric.)

CHORIC

And he went all over the Jordan Valley proclaiming baptism
as the mark of repentance and of the forgiveness of sins . . .

> The voice of one
> crying in the wilderness,
> > Prepare ye the way of the Lord,
> > make his paths straight.

After me comes one who is mightier than I.
I am not fit to unfasten his shoes.
I have baptized you with water.
He will baptize you with the Holy Spirit.

> Then Jesus came from Galilee
> > and was baptized by John
> > in the Jordan.

> At the moment
> when he came out of the water,
> > he saw
> > the heaven split open,
> and the Spirit
> coming down upon him like a dove
> > and

a voice from heaven
was heard:
You are my dearly loved Son,
in whom I am well pleased.
Shortly after
he called a few men
to follow him.
And they went into Capernaum;
and straightway on the Sabbath day
he entered into the synagogue and taught.
And they were astonished
at his doctrine;
for he taught them as one who had authority,
and not as the scribes.
And there was
in their synagogue
a man
with an unclean spirit;
and he cried out saying . . .

*(During the brief recorded sequence, the
Choric assumes stance of onlookers with
fear, stunned surprise, and awe among their
reactions.)*

AUDIO RECORDED SEQUENCE

*(FADE IN over last Choric lines—sounds of
commotion, running fast, hard-breathing,
urgent voices . . .)*

MANY VOICES
. . . hold him, his arms, someone take his arms . . .

VOICE OF THE POSSESSED

(Overlaying all other sounds.)

Let us alone. We know you. Jesus of Nazareth!

MANY VOICES

(Hard-breathing and urgent voices but more subdued than above . . .)

. . . hold him fast, loop it, quickly, the other end, there, tie it, outside now . . .

VOICE OF THE POSSESSED

(A loud shrieking cry.)

. . . you shall not bind me . . . Jesus. . . !

MANY VOICES

(With gasps and surprise.)

. . . the ropes dangling, shredded, he has broken the . . .

VOICE OF THE POSSESSED

. . . WHAT DO YOU WANT WITH US, JESUS OF NAZARETH? Have you come to destroy us? We know who you are—who you are—the Holy One of God!

JESUS' VOICE

(Controlled but firmly in command.)

Silence! Hold your tongue! Be silent and—get out of him. OUT!

(Sounds of thrashing about, breathing, moaning, and/or guttural grunts. Suddenly, a loud cry and the harsh, gasping breathing subsides)

MANY VOICES
(A hubbub of sound—with great surprise and astonishment.)
What new thing is this?
Never before have we seen . . .
What has happened?
What is this?
Yahweh was here!
. . . in the Name of the Almighty!
A new kind of teaching, this.
He speaks with authority.
Look, the possessed is at peace!
When he gives orders, even the evil spirits obey him!
(NOTE: Great care must be exercised in the staging of this scene so the sound effects do not exceed bounds of good taste—probably best underplayed.)

NARRATOR
The news spread rapidly, about the man in the synagogue who was cleansed of an evil spirit. Soon Jesus was being spoken of all over the district of Galilee.

(End of AUDIO RECORDED SEQUENCE)

CHORIC
Who is this man
who strikes down Lucifer
with a Holy Word
uttered
in blaze of clashing wills;
who says to his underlings
demons—OUT!
. . . you may no longer live
in human habitation!

Who is this man
    who brings to the battleground
        of human heart
        and mind
            his desert victory!

*(LIGHTS FADE on Choric. LIGHTS UP
on Marcus.)*

MARCUS

Strange happenings these! First a voice from heaven saying to this Jesus of Nazareth, you are my Son, my beloved. I am well pleased with you. Then, shortly after, the unclean spirit cried out and called Jesus, Holy One of God. Every time Simon told the mother and me what was happening, I wrote more—mostly questions at first. For a long time I was like the blind man, crying for sight. Later, I saw only men like trees walking.

So much of what Jesus taught denied every devout expectation. He seemed to be speaking of another—oh, I near forgot! One other thing fueled my writing.

Long before I knew what they meant, some words of Jesus struck me, stuck in my memory like a prickly burr to a woolen tunic. It was the announcement he made: "The time has come at last! The kingdom of God has arrived . . ."

(LIGHTS OUT ABRUPTLY.)

Just Like That

(LIGHTS FLARE UP brightly with first line.)

CHORIC

Just like that
Jesus of Nazareth
      walks out of the desert
      into Galilee
      and announces:
it's here
the kingdom of God
is here!
   like he had brought it
   with him
      as if he himself
      embodied
      the kingdom—
           he said
you must change
   your hearts
   and minds
   and believe the good news:
it's here
the kingdom of God
is here;

                              you must change
                              your hearts
                              and minds
                which are convinced
                the kingdom
                was or will be;
                                        you
                                        must
                                        change
                                        and

stop living in a noble history
where the only reality is
the past tense;
                                        you
                                        must
                                        change
                                        and

stop living in the futile speculation
about a future
which is fully in the hand of God—
            a future
            which is always beyond now—
a future which
can never be
a present reality—
            or if it is . . .
                        (a present reality)
            . . . is not future!
                                        you
                                        must
                                        change
                                        and

believe the good news—
>> it's here
>> the kingdom of God
>> is here

>>>>>>>>>>>> *Now*

>> believe the good news
>> God's kingdom is here

That seems to be the message:
>>>>>>>> the kingdom
>>>>>>>> came in
>>>>>>>> with Jesus,
>>>>> the kingdom
>>>>> is
>>>>> where Jesus is;
you must change
>> your hearts
>> and minds
>> and believe the good news.

>>>>>> *who is this man*

>>>>>>>> *who*

>>>> *walks out of the desert*
>>>> *into Galilee*
>>>> *and announces—*
it's here
the kingdom of God
is here
>>>>>> *(LIGHTS FADE.)*

EARLY CONFLICT—
JESUS AND THE PHARISEES

Healing of the Paralytic
Vignette

(House of AMASAI—Pharisee. ELIEL and AMASAI in conversation about the Law.)

ELIEL

I tell you, Amasai, the time has come to fix more firmly in the hearts of the people every jot and tittle of the Law of Yahweh.

AMASAI

You are still convinced there is a falling away?

ELIEL

(Emphatically.)

More than ever! An ignoring of the feast days. Too much levity at the last Passover. And among us those who do little more than dampen their fingertips before they sit to meat. There is no respect . . .

AMASAI

How would you change? Do we not teach the Law and circumscribe the pathway upon which the faithful walk?

ELIEL

We do. But, among us, we must require—nay, demand—

rigid obedience. Otherwise . . .

> *(His gestures show he means the less obedient will be cast out.)*

AMASAI

Among the people?

ELIEL

There is a rabble which keeps the people in turmoil. They must be . . .

> *(Hands are clapped sharply in greeting outside of the house. AMASAI rises as AARON, LEVI, and JOEL enter.)*

AMASAI

Peace be unto you. Will you . . .

> *(He points to stools but the three are obviously too angry and distraught to sit. They wave him back to his chair. He sits, uncertainly, as JOEL begins to speak.)*

JOEL

He is out there again—stirring up the people.

AMASAI

He?

LEVI

The carpenter from Nazareth.

AARON

We have just come from . . .

JOEL

. . . the house of Adonijah . . .

LEVI

. . . near the sea, by the watering trough.

AMASAI

Jesus of Nazareth?

AARON, LEVI, JOEL
(In concert, more or less.)

The same.

AARON

. . . with a few of the fisherfolk who follow him about.

JOEL

He was in the way . . .

LEVI

. . . we had word that Adonijah had bade him come . . .

AARON

. . . so we walked by. The servant of Adonijah ran after us to bid us enter. The Teacher from Nazareth was coming.

JOEL
(With a knowing glance around the circle.)

We did not decline.

ELIEL

You came in distraught. Did the carpenter arrive?

AARON

He did—and quickly a multitude gathered.

LEVI

. . . pressed into the house. There was no more room to receive them . . .

AARON

. . . milling at the door. Tight-packed.

AMASAI

Did he speak?

AARON

He did. About a new kingdom,

JOEL

It was not what he said about—(*Pause, with disdain.*)—about his new kingdom.

LEVI

The people were in a frenzy after—after he . . .

ELIEL

. . . after he?

JOEL

Were it not that these eyes had seen and these ears had heard, I would not . . .

LEVI

. . . we were seated as he taught . . .

AARON

. . . there were voices at the door. It seemed some wanted to enter. But no one gave way.

JOEL

In a few minutes, even as he spoke, from overhead some chipped mortar fell on our heads. There above us . . .

AARON

. . . men were lifting the tiles.

JOEL

... suddenly, there before our eyes, they were letting down—
it was Reuben, son of Shimei. Him with the palsy, these ten
years. He no longer could walk. They let down his bed with
ropes—he lying upon it—before him from Nazareth . . .

AARON

. . . before the carpenter . . .

JOEL

. . . he looked upon him, then up at the broken roof where the
four men waited. Then he stretched out his hand and said to
Reuben—him with the palsy:"Son, thy sins be forgiven thee."

(AMASAI and ELIEL start noticeably.)

ELIEL

He said . . .

AARON

. . . he did. Thy sins are forgiven!

JOEL

I could not believe such blasphemy had come to my ears and
thought to myself—who can forgive sins but God only . . .

LEVI

. . . and I thought likewise!

AMASAI

Did he say more?

JOEL

(Holding up his hand.)
He did. He turned and looked at us—the three of us . . .

AARON

. . . at none other. Just the three of us . . .

JOEL

. . . and he said, "Why reason ye these things in your hearts? Which is easier? To say to this man . . ."

LEVI

. . . he said, which is easier . . .

JOEL

. . . to say to this man: Thy sins are forgiven or Take up thy bed and walk . . .

AARON
(Throwing up his hands.)
. . . what could we say?

LEVI

. . . he was making sport of us.

ELIEL
(To AMASAI.)
I spoke of the rabble. He must be stopped!

JOEL

He turned full on us . . .

AARON

. . . just the three of us. He spoke to us! There was no mistaking it . . .

JOEL

. . . and said, That ye may know the Son of man hath power to forgive sins—then, then he laid his hand on him with the palsy and spoke—"Arise, take up thy bed and walk."

AARON
He turned—we watched—Reuben turned on his side, pulled
his knees to his chest and rolled over . . .

JOEL
. . . and stood to his feet. Then—then he picked up his pallet
and walked. . . .

LEVI
. . . the crowd made way . . .

AARON
. . . we have just come from there . . .

LEVI
. . . the people were in a frenzy. They cried out hosanna . . .

JOEL
(Spits it out.)
Blasphemer.

ELIEL
(To AMASAI.)
This Jesus is a troublemaker. He subverts the Law. Only his
blood will stop the turmoil among the people—this foolish-
ness . . .

AMASAI
. . . the man walked.

JOEL
By some magic. He hath Beelzebub!

ELIEL
He takes the people from following the Law . . .

AARON

.. and sits at meat with publicans and sinners . . .

JOEL

. . . one day I saw a harlot touch him. He just looked at her. He did not turn nor strike her hand away . . .

LEVI

. . . on that day . . .

AARON

. . . when he sat at meat with the publicans . . .

LEVI

. . . we spoke to his disciples but Jesus answered and said, They that are whole have no need of the physician, but they that are sick: I came not to call the righteous but sinners to repentance . . .

JOEL

. . . always sharp with his answers. We cannot catch him.

LEVI

. . . he said, New wine must be put into new bottles. No man putteth new wine into old bottles, else the new wine doth burst the old bottles and the wine is spilled. Neither doth any man sew a piece of new cloth on an old garment, else the new piece rendeth the old.

JOEL

It is clear. He is a rabble-rouser. He seeks to bring a new order . . .

ELIEL

. . . and will destroy the old.

JOEL

Already I see his way—he puts first the whining needs of the common ones. He destroys our customs to—to heal on the Sabbath.

ELIEL

He speaks against the Law.

JOEL

He is a blasphemer. He turns upside down the old ways. He tricks the people—they turn from us to follow him.

ELIEL

As I said—the old must stand. New wine, he says, must not be spilled. We shall see—what shall be spilled.

> *(This segment may conclude with the Pharisees standing—postured dogma—in one fixed position or, in sequential poses pantomiming reaction to the action. If desired, HOLD pose or poses for duration of the RECORDED AUDIO SEQUENCE which follows.)*

Man with the Withered Hand

(The mood here is a bit flip/hip to contrast with the formal character of the pantomime poses. This may be an AUDIO RE-CORDED SEQUENCE or the entire scene could be done from another part of the stage or from a raised vantage point in the audience.)

CHORIC

Jesus entered again into the synagogue
    and there was a man
    there
    who had a withered hand.
           And they watched him—
           (that's what the Word says . . .)
           —they watched him;
    the Pharisees were there:
    "Careful now, Jesus;
        don't you dare
        drop
        any customs—
            they
            could
            break

                                        —or give up
                                    some of our traditions
                                            they're
                                            sacred,
                                            you know
                                    —as for the Law
                                            let's just
                                            fulfil it
                                            the old way!"
                        They were there
                        they watched him—
        whether he would heal, that is,
        whether he would heal on the Sabbath!
                . . . the man had a withered hand
                he couldn't use his withered hand
                and he wanted healing for his withered hand
        so Jesus
        he said
        to the man with the withered hand
                        step up here
                                    and
                                    the man
                                    stepped
                                    up.
        Then Jesus
        looked around
        —and
        around—
                                at all of those men
                                watching there
                                        to see

whether he would heal on the Sabbath
and he said—
(that's right! He
looked right at
the Pharisees
watching him there,
and he said)—

you tell me!
is it right
to do good on the Sabbath day
or to do evil?
is it right
to save life
or to kill?

That's
what he said,
and
the Word says . . .

. . . there was a dead silence

a dead silence
they had nothing to say.
Jesus
looked
at the Pharisees
—sad and angry—

He could tell
they didn't care about the people
—only that
not a single Law
be broken.

> He was sad and angry
> and he said
> to the man—
"Stretch out your hand."
He did—
and glory hallelujah
the hand was healed
> glory hallelujah
> the hand was healed
> > glory hallelujah
> > the hand was healed
—perfect
like the other!

> The Pharisees
> had blood in their eye
> when they left
> the synagogue
> that day;
they started to plot
with the Herodians
how they could get rid of Jesus.
Who is this man
> hunted by the very men
> who should have
> welcomed him?

SECRETS ARE FOR TELLING

Hidden Seed—Certain Harvest

(Choric members will be arranged antiphonally, at first. The joyous, lilting mood of one group will be in sharp contrast with the staid and skeptical rejoinders of the other group.)

(LIGHTS—SPOT on each.)

CHORIC

The King Has Come . . .
> Just like that
> Jesus of Nazareth
>> walks out of the desert
>> into Galilee
> and announces:

it's here;
the kingdom of God
is here!

>> . . . it can't be!
>> Not yet. But it will
>> come. The Blest One
>> has promised . . .

It's here
—now

                                        . . . God's kingdom?
                                        Not yet! We can't see
                                        a throne or a king . . .

The kingdom is here

                                        . . . impossible. It
                                        must be hidden . . .

Hidden, perhaps
—but here.

                                        . . . we'd rather believe
                                        the word of our fathers,
                                        God's kingdom will come . . .

Not only future—
          is arriving!
          is here!

                                        . . . a kingdom?
                                        No throne? A king
                                        and no pomp? It
                                        can't be . . .

     . . . just like that
     Jesus of Nazareth
               walks out of the desert
               into Galilee
               and announces;
     The kingdom of God is here
               . . . like he had brought it
     with him
                    as if he himself
                    embodied
                    the kingdom!

That seems to be the message . . .
     . . . the king
     has
     come
     and brought his kingdom
     along
              . . . the kingdom
              came in
              with Jesus
                    . . . the kingdom
                    is
                    where Jesus is!
You must change
     your hearts
     and minds
     and believe this good news.
              (PAUSE—LIGHTS BUILD to FULL—
              drowning the SPOTS.)

     . . . a new day has dawned . . .
                    who is he?
                    who is this man?
              why is the mystery
              locked away?
     when will we know . . .

NARRATOR
And Jesus said to the disciples:
     to you has been given
     the secret
     of the kingdom of God . . .
              be careful how you listen.

CHORIC
>> who is he?
>> who is this man?
>> why is the mystery
>> locked away?
> when will we know . . .

I want *you* to know;
> the devils know
> and shout my name!
>> the Gentiles hear
>> and somehow
>> believe!

I want *you* to understand . . .
>> to *you* has been given
>> the secret
>> of the kingdom of God.
>> . . . be careful!
>> be careful
>> how you listen . . .

A sower went out to sow . . .
> steadily
> trudging
> rhythmically
> casting
the seed from his arc-ing arm
>> sturdily
>> swinging
>> repeatedly
>> flinging

a curtain of grains to the ground below
a curtain of grains to the ground below
hard beaten
and rocky
brambled with thorns
a curtain of grains to the ground below
hear well!
are you listening?
is the mystery clear?
a curtain of grains on the ground below
deep loamy
and fertile
receptive and warm
a curtain of grains to the ground below
some lost to the birds
some scorched by the sun
some choked by the thorns
but some—
deeply held in the shade and the loam
—came bursting to life
and brought forth rich bounty
a curtain of grains from the ground below
Hear well!
Are you listening?
Is the mystery clear?

NARRATOR

Then he said to them:
"Is a lamp brought into the room to be put under a bucket or
underneath the bed? Surely its place is on the lampstand!
There is nothing hidden which is not meant to be made

perfectly plain one day, and there are no secrets which are not meant one day to be common knowledge. If a man has ears, he should use them."

CHORIC
>Hear well!
>
>Are you listening?
>
>Is the mystery clear?

Before certain harvest
>—comes seed time
>—hidden seed time
>—always seed time
>>Do you hear . . .

. . . for this
I have come;
The kingdom is here.

HINTS OF IDENTITY

Introduction: Trumpeted but Hidden
Narration, Choric, and Music

Jesus showed himself Lord over:
        Nature——Simon Peter in the Storm
        Demons——The Gadarene Set Free
        Disease——Judith: Healed of a Hemorrhage
        Death——Daughter of Jairus: Raised to Life

NARRATOR

There were many witnesses of Jesus-acts. Each time Jesus met someone and filled their need, he seemed to win a follower. Some of the Jesus-acts were called miracles. Wherever he went, for months, he was thronged by the multitudes—a few who, in truth, heard his message of another kingdom, some who needed the touch of his hand and others—others whose habit it was, simply spoken, to follow crowds.

But few, if any, understood that the acts of Jesus-power actually became a stumbling-block to understanding—the understanding that his coming had another purpose.

CHORIC
Who is this man
                announcing
a new kingdom-—

       its secret shaped and cloaked
       in the tantalizing mystery
       of earthy tales?
       . . . a new kingdom—

       its power
       pulsing beneath the sheath of tradition
       stretching the forms
       held sacred for centuries.
       . . . a new kingdom—
           its new king
           unsettling the cornerstones
           tipping the plumbline
           askew
           . . . a new kingdom—
its message
hidden deep
except to those who hear
except to those with ears to hear
       the word of full disclosure
       —who this man is!
         anon
       that word is trumpeted:
           by demons
           cast rigid in fear
           by his superior place.
           . . . trumpeted:
by Gentile
delivered through his power
and brought to peace.
       . . . trumpeted:

by voice from out a cloud
speaking clear,
its heavenly confirmation
                . . . trumpeted:
    but hidden
    except to those who—
                unbound
                freed from the prison
                of their faithless past
                and given sight
        —rise
    to herald his kingship.
Thus taught,
        they follow in the way
        of his new kingdom
                or,
                with stopped ears,
                they stumble on in blindness!

        *(CHORIC HOLDS FINAL POSE from
        last three lines in introduction IN
        SILENCE.)*

        *(SUDDENLY
        BRASS WITH ELECTRIC BASS
        GUITAR—begin raucous, wild—MUSIC
        for first stanza of "Master, the Tempest Is
        Raging"* . . . then second stanza, muted but
        with the same urgent tone and beat as sug-
        gested by the words in the first stanza.
        When muted music begins . . .)*

**Life Songs, No. 2*, page 219

CHORIC (or SINGLE VOICE)

. . .and the same day,
when the even was come,
		he saith unto them,
Let us pass over unto the other side.

And when they had sent away the multitude
they took him even as he was in the ship
		And there were also
		with him
		other little ships.
And there arose
a great storm
of wind,
		and the waves
		beat into the ship
		so that
		it was now full.

And he was in the hinder part
		of the ship
				asleep
				on a pillow . . .

		(PAUSE—as long as necessary to synchro-
		nize words with music.)

and they awake him,
and say unto him,

VOICES IN SONG
(Could be solo, quartet, or chorus.)

Master, the tempest is raging!
The billows are tossing high!
The sky is o'ershadowed with blackness,
No shelter or help is nigh;
Carest thou not that we perish?
How canst thou lie asleep.
When each moment so madly is threat'ning
A grave in the angry deep?

*(LIGHTS and MUSIC FADE SLOWLY
AS SPOT COMES UP on Simon Peter.)*

NOTE: The four monologues dealing with acts of Jesus' power over nature, demons, disease, and death form a powerful cluster which, taken together, may acutally inhibit or distort understanding of Jesus' real purpose in coming. Accordingly, to maintain a proper spatial balance within the complete message, consideration may be given to dropping one or more of the monologues from a full-length production. Or, through narrative comment or other means, recognition could be given to the major focus in Mark's Gospel on the way of obedience and discipleship.

The Wind and the Waves Obey

(Simon Peter in the Storm)
Monologue

I am known as Simon, the fisherman.

'Tis only a short trip—a little over six miles—from Capernaum to Gergesa. That is, if there's a brisk wind for the sail, and from the right quarter. An hour or two. Or all night, rowing, if the sea's against you.

That afternoon we had wind—a stiff sou'wester. After we started, it veered—sou' by sou'west. The sea came up in a hurry, faster than usual. There were three other boats; we left about the same time, stayed close.

We weren't too far from Gergesa; I could make out water pots sitting on a few rooftops. Andrew had lashed the sail. Three of us on the rudder bar, the tiller, couldn't hold her into the cresting waves. They were vicious—higher than the boat was long. Cresting three ways at once.

Andrew and Judas were with me on the tiller. Thomas and Philip—and Matthew—were bailing, with great swings of their leather buckets. But the water was rising.

The Master sat midship—toward the hinder part. He seemed to be asleep.

The others were with James and John—in the boat to our left; close enough for us to see they were out of control. Their mast had snapped before they furled the sail; now it dangled and swung like a club of death each time the bow went down in the trough.

We were all fighting for our lives; and in our boat, three on the tiller bar! It would swing one way wide. Then, when a wave twisted us sharp away, swung back—bruising us sore on arms and ribs.

Andrew was gasping for breath. I could tell, he was near the end of his strength. Judas, thick and solid like an ox, was silent except for deep and rhythmic grunts. Every muscle in his back and arms bulged and rippled with the straining. Of a sudden I caught a sob in my own throat—the kind wrenched out of you without your say-so, when you need more strength and there is no whit left.

Unless the wind abated, I knew we would go down—and that in sight of a near-shore. I looked again at Jesus, sitting quietly, his back to the mast. I listened to the warping of the boards on the fo'c's'le—against each other—never had I heard that before. I heard the screaming of the wind through the rigging, and heaved—three of us heaved against the sea trying to wrest the rudder from us.

In that instant, the tiller bar snapped. All three of us were thrown against the starboard gun'l. And in that instant, clutching the broken piece in my hand, I shouted to the quiet one, still asleep—

"Master, don't you care? We perish!"

Our little craft veered and tipped like a drunken sailor. I can see it yet. Jesus looked up, put one hand on the mast—I watched him—stood, spread his feet against the roll, raised his right hand, high, and shouted into the howling wind—I heard him—Peace! Then more quietly—be still.

There are no words. I cannot tell what or how. Only that, in an instant, all was suddenly calm—no wind, no waves and we began drifting on the gentle water, in a circle, that is until we lashed a spare tiller bar to the broken stub.

As we wound the rope I heard Judas muttering under his breath, "What manner of man is this, that even the wind and the waves obey him?"

Peace, Be Still

(MUSIC UP—refrain only—muted.)

CHORIC
. . . and he arose

> and rebuked the wind,
> and said unto the sea

PEACE, be still,

> And the wind ceased,
> and there was a great calm,
> . . . and he said
> unto them,
> why are ye so fearful?
> how is it that ye have
> no faith?

And they feared exceedingly,

> and said
> one to another,
> What manner of man is this,
> that even the wind
> and the sea obey him?

I Was There
Monologue

(LIGHTS UP on . . .)

MARCUS

I was there. Perhaps that was when my book actually began . . .

(Pause for remembering.)

. . . you will remember my earlier words—that our olive press was the cause of my first sight of Jesus from Nazareth.

In the country of the Gadarenes, to the far north, there was an ironworker, Arodi by name. His skill was noised abroad throughout all the land. Three times, in the season past, the main shaft had broken—the heavy spindle which holds the press for the turning. The mother was firm—before the next pressing, we must put in a new spindle and it must be crafted by Arodi.

She bid me join a caravan to Capernaum, bring greetings to Simon her kinsman, then hire a ship to Gergesa, where Arodi had his iron works.

Simon was not at home, only his wife and her mother. She knew not where he was; only that he had left with the carpenter from Nazareth. Since the sun was still high I decided to carry my burden at once to Arodi, then return on the morrow for some days while he cast the spindle.

I found a ship, lashed the iron shaft to the mast—the two broken pieces to show Arodi the form—and we hoisted sail. Until the sail was trimmed, we came close on land to a multitude. The shipowner called to me and asked if I had heard of the Nazareth carpenter, Jesus. I nodded and he pointed.

I could see one standing among a large crowd—Simon must have been among them. The sound of his voice came to us, but no meaning until, of a sudden just as we turned, the brisk breeze setting us on our course also brought his words clearly across the water—"The kingdom of God is like this. A man scatters seed on the land; he goes to bed at night and gets up in the morning . . . the seed sprouts and grows—how, he does not know. The earth produces a crop without help from anyone: first a blade, then the ear of corn, then the full-grown grain in the ear. . . ." Then the wind veered a bit and carried us beyond the hearing.

The boatman spoke to the wind, "You're a hearty helper (and to me)—there'll be a storm before the sun is gone, mark me!"

The sun was high still and the little ship fairly scudded. Perhaps I could finish and return this day to Simon's house. But when I asked the boatman, he just grunted and said, "Come when you're finished, we shall see," with an ominous look at the sky.

I found the ironworks straightway—near to the fish sheds. I heard, before I saw, the great roaring fire. Arodi I found also. He sent two men with donkeys to pick up the broken spindle. In less than an hour I had showed him how we wished the new shaft to be formed. He bade me return on the eighth day.

The sun was low when I stepped into the boat. The boatman just shook his head and pointed to the black clouds. Then he said, "Too much white on the water. Perhaps when the moon comes out it will quiet and we can cast off." He went on. "Look yonder."

I sighted along his arm and saw boats—four or five, I couldn't be sure—tossed like boards on the sea.

"They're in trouble. This evening's sea has a demon." I remember still, I was impatient. But even as I watched the long hour grow into a strange black sunset streaked with pale lemon, the storm grew worse. The craft were closer now—there were four—but that only added to the terror, for we could see they were often not able to keep headed into the sea and seemed near to being swamped.

Brackish clouds raced against the far horizon. Only a sliver of sick roiling gray light from the setting sun showed now against the mountains behind us.

I ate some goat cheese and bread as we waited, bobbing sharply even at our inner mooring.

Suddenly the evening dark was shredded and sheeted by lightning from mountains to sea and in the same instant the wind fell dead! The boatman stood, perplexity written on his brow. He held his cheek high to feel the wind and turned to me, "Never, in thirty years, have I seen the like. Not a breath of air!"

Indeed, the ships so recently near sinking were lying motionless. They were near enough, even in the spent light, we could see men bailing, then shipping oars and begin to row.

I shall never forget the next few moments. Without a word, yet thinking the same thought, the boatman and I stepped out on the sand. As they came close to shore, I saw with a start that Simon and some of his friends were in the lead boat. The carpenter from Nazareth also. Simon jumped into the water—near to his chest it was—and drew the boat toward a piling in shallow water, looped the rope with a deft double twist and walked toward me, altogether ignoring the others who stepped into the water behind him.

Simon was white with fright. He gave no sign that he knew me nor any that he did not know me. His eyes were wide; his lips quivered. As if with the ague, his shoulders and arms shook. He grasped both my elbows in the clench of his hands and pushed his face close to mine—though his eyes were unseeing. His voice was hoarse; the words seemed to twist out of his mouth. "The wind stopped at his word! The waves were still! The wind stopped. . . ." the last sound trailed and dangled. He stared past me. And he dropped his hands, turning and stumbling a bit before his sight seemed to focus and he followed the others.

Who Is This Man?—Preamble

CHORIC
Who is this man?
        —the wind lies still
        upon his sharp rebuke,
                the roiling stops
                the waves at rest!
Who is this man
        who stands and speaks?
        . . . who speaks
        as if by his word
the worlds are held together;
        this man
                whose call
                commands
                the elements?
        this man
                who orders peace!
        Who is this man
                announcing
a new kingdom
himself as king
        each act of power
        shaped towards a single end:
        to tell his name,

     his earthly purpose
     and to show the way into
his new kingdom
himself as king?

NARRATOR

And they came over
     unto the other side of the sea
     into the country of the Gadarenes.
And when he was come out of the ship

     immediately
     there met him out of the tombs
     a man with an unclean spirit . . .

The Gadarene Set Free
(A Man from the Tombs)
Monologue

My story is brief.

Much of my life I do not remember. I was told by them who saw it, I dwelt once in the tombs. No man would have me in his dwelling. That I was bound by chains which my raging strength would rend asunder. That anon I cut myself with stones. That in the quiet nighttime hours my curdling screams would fright the babes in their mother's arms—far distant.

None of this do I remember. Only long ago and at the end— just before Jesus healed me and gave me a new mind.

I do have a clouded image of my child-home, of a mother timid and fearful, of a father who struck and beat and shouted at us all. Who chased away the shreds of peace we'd gather in the hours he was away feeding the swine. Who brought to our house each eventide great waves of sour fear.

And I remember—like a tale told me long ago—the hate. First fear, then hate, nurtured by each vicious blow. Anger that boiled until, as a lad, I could think of naught but that, some night, I would take the knife to his throat and be done with this fearsome noise.

That was not to be.

One dark day he came home and found me lining pictures in

the dust. He stopped for a moment, then slashed his sandal through my markings and thundered loud—"What mischief make you here, marking pictures in the dust? Graven images. Why are you not out gathering straw?" He spit upon the ground. "Graven images! Your hide shall learn its lesson."

Before I could breathe to answer, he had set upon me, threw me to the ground, took his lash—fixed to a rod for swine— and cut my face. The blood blinded me in an instant and I turned, writhing, only to feel the heavy rod on my head at the back.

I knew my cheek was on the bloodied dust. I knew the blows upon my legs and back. Then another to the head. And of a sudden, in the same instant that its pain pierced deep, a strange warm flowed around my skull to the brow. And a wondrous light did shine a thousand times.

That is the last I remember. Except—except every night I had a dream of lifting a great body above my head and flinging it against the wall. Then all would be dark again.

Until one day—a ship was tied along the shore . . . I could see it well. A stranger with a little band stepped from it. A few others joined them, from another ship.

There had been a storm. All through the violent wrenching of the screaming wind I had run across the rocks, tumbling, hurting, stumbling, running—and all the time laughing with loud, unnatural glee.

Then, of a sudden, all was still. I cowered. Deep in me I felt a certain knowledge that power had come upon power—and I trembled.

I watched them as they stood beside the sea. Saw several landsmen cluster for a time, then the stranger and his band walked up the path past where I hid.

A thousand storms inside wrenched me sore. The trembling hurled me to the ground each time I stood.

He came closer.

My body wracked this way and that. A thousand voices cried out. I heard these voices say, Son of God, and I fell down. Other words I heard as well but they are gone. Except for three. In the midst of a great and violent thrashing of my body against the jagged rocks there came into the tearing of my flesh and the wild screams I knew somehow came from my own throat—there came three words: Peace be still.

To this day, those are wondrous words.

For in that moment I felt a great inner rending and lay limp upon the rocks. He took my hand and raised me up.

I knew I was whole.

I begged him to let me walk with him. He looked with love upon me, then said, "Go home to thy friends. Tell them how great things the Lord hath done for thee."

He paused a moment as I embraced his feet. Then a little wistfully—it seemed to me—he said, "They will hear."

NARRATOR
And when Jesus was passed over again
       by ship to the other side

                    . . . behold,

            there cometh

            one of the rulers of the synagogue,

                    Jairus by name,

            who besought him greatly,

My little daughter lieth at the point of death:

. . . come and lay thy hands on her,

that she may be healed . . .

                    and

                    Jesus went with him.

And a certain woman

which had an issue of blood twelve years . . .

(In Mark 5, the story of the woman healed of an issue of blood is "sandwiched" into the story of the raising of Jairus' daughter, Dramatically, this is also valid, if the two persons portraying these characters are sufficiently skilled. However, since the stories are presented here in monologue form rather than in vignette form, the presentation of each monologue in its entirety and in sequence as given is in order.)

No Bondage Now–I'm Free

(Judith: Healed of a Hemorrhage)
Monologue

My name is Judith.

I have this day been freed of bondage—a bondage of blood.

You will pardon me. I said, this day. Of a truth, it is now years. But each new day the joy of deliverance is so great and the memory so fresh that when I speak of the miracle it seems as if it took place this very noon-day.

The sun was high that day when I followed the crowd on the rocky road into town. The streets were narrow and, filled with people.

But—pardon again—I hurry ahead of my story.

Near ten years after I became a maiden there came this loathsome burden, without warning—a constant issue of blood. At first I was frightened, then impatient, then angry and sick at heart.

Why should I carry this mark? Why should I be cut off from my fellows with whisperings and averted gaze? Why should my desire for a husband be thwarted by this shame? The questions haunted me.

Had I sinned even in my innocent years? Was I perchance the

child of some great sin? Why should I be the one to feel so much weight of the Law in all the necessary rituals?

Many days I cried out my helpless hurt. Every hour I muttered my loathing.

I grew to hate the prison of my disease. Each morning I woke happy but only for a moment; quickly the weight of my illness settled on my chest like a nether millstone. Every evening I prayed for death to free me from this sign that set me apart. All day, every day, in all the hours, I was not free of the judgment against me.

I suffered many things from the physicians. With cutting and herbs and charms they tried to stanch the flow. My living I spent with them. Until there was no more. I refused to beg. But my labor for hire was always interrupted by weakness.

By turn I shook my fist at Yahweh and besought him to have mercy. By turn I prayed and cursed. By turn I hoped and lay in the trough of despair.

Then I heard of a prophet—Jesus of Nazareth—who had brought healing to some. Three times, in Capernaum, he came near where I was. Three times I left my house to find him, to beg for his mercy. Three times I fought through the crowd around him to come close only to have weakness overtake me—and the crowd would pass on with him in the center.

I was near death in my spirit. The days crushed my hope, for I was getting worse, instead of better. The nights hid my tears. Only the coverlet on my pillow, hung out to dry each morning, was true companion in my misery.

Then a neighbor child rushed in—"The prophet is back! He goes to the house of Jairus"—and was gone.

Quickly I wrapped my cloak about me. My feet became wings. My hopes soared higher than the rooftops. Until I saw the multitude. I could look down from the hilltop street at the crowd coming up. I was determined not to move until he passed my way.

The press of bodies was great. I flattened myself against a doorway to keep from being swept ahead of the crowd. When I saw him tall a few cubits before me I bent my shoulder into the human mass. In the center was he whom I must implore for healing. Around him were some they called his disciples. I knew this must be the time. I wanted to call but who was I among the hundreds. So I bit my lip and pushed hard. The heavy weakness began to come in waves. I cried in my heart to Yahweh for strength.

The crowd moved on—the turmoil of bodies constantly shifting. Could I reach him? Already the press from behind had moved him past me.

Perhaps—if I could only touch his clothes, I would be made whole.

Frantically I clawed at the tunics ahead of me but there was no opening. Then I bent and discovered the press was less near the ground. I stood erect once more to glimpse his place, then bent and plunged and touched the hem of his garment. I clung to it with my fingers, for a moment, as I felt feet lifting around me.

In that moment he stopped. I heard a voice. "Who touched my clothes?"

I let go. I knew I was healed.

One of his disciples said, "You see the multitude thronging around you and yet you ask, who touched me?"

Fear at my boldness tore at my heart. But a greater joy overwhelmed my being—even to the trembling. Fear and joy together forced my tongue and I spoke. "It was I, Master!" The crowd gave way as I knelt at his feet. "I touched you."

Then he said the words that embraced me with warm, "Daughter, your faith has made you whole; go in peace and be rid of your plague."

I kissed his feet, looked for a moment into his eyes, then, minding not the crowd, I pressed through to the edge and ran. I ran, with strength and joy, to my house, to the inner court.

There I wept.

Tears of thanksgiving and praise.

I have this day been freed of bondage!

No Final Prison Here
(Daughter of Jairus: Raised to Life)
Monologue

It is now five years—almost six—this summer solstice past. I was twelve when, of a sudden, I fell ill of a fever.

Nine days the fever raged. On the fifth I could no longer walk. The physicians were baffled. All they knew, of a certainty, was that the fever must be held down.

All the water I could drink. No less than each hour—tea from the bark of juniper. At the last I could not sit to drink. My father, Jairus—a ruler of the synagogue—sat by and with a small wooden ladle tipped the tea between my lips. Hour after hour.

And water from the spring. All day cousin Tamar carried the cool water so mother could place the chilling wet linens along my side and across my chest. After a time I could not tell when the fresh linens were thrust against me—there was no change—all felt the same, sodden and hot.

On the morning of the ninth day—Mother tells me—my senses left me and I lay as dead, but breathing. It was then, she said, my father went to seek him from Nazareth—Jesus, the worker of miracles. I had only heard his name and that many followed after; also that the Pharisees were sore displeased.

Father thought better of him, believed him to be a messenger from the Blessed One. Perhaps even the Messiah, although he could not understand why, if this was he, he did not call all the people to rise up against the Romans.

I have no memory of my father leaving, or how long he was gone. Only of a fleeting awareness of those that stood nearby. And of my mother, seated, stroking my forehead, her tears dropping on my bosom. I could feel them when they touched and remember that, on my burning skin, they felt cool.

Mother says my eyes were always open; of that I do not know.

Suddenly, I seemed fully awake. I felt a strange rippling across my body, a numbness in my feet and arms, then spreading upward and inward as if my body was being folded up, from the outside in. I remember thinking *there is air for only three more breaths, breathe slowly.* I did. On the third—it was large and deep—Mother started, placed her cheek against my nostrils and her thumb on my wrist.

In that same instant, I felt a tiny lurching and when I looked again, there lay my body, below me to the left, I can see it well, even today.

Mother looked around at my cousins, shook her head, then placed her hand on my breast, pressed hard. I could see her shift the hand, searching for the familiar beat. Then she slowly pulled the sheet up over my face, stood and turned to her brother, my uncle Ben-hadad. "Her spirit is gone." He took her in his arms as she let the sobs come.

I heard them all as I looked down on the room; full it was with kinsfolk. I heard the first wail of mourning. And I heard the words, "Send to Jairus, no longer to trouble the healer."

I remember thinking—is this death? I seemed to be more alive than ever. The fever was gone. A great peace enveloped me.

It seemed odd to be there watching. There was a turmoil of movement inside and outside the house. I could see both. Little clusters of people weeping. A scurrying here and there. Then suddenly—a commotion at the gate.

From the center of the group that halted there stepped a man. He motioned three other men to follow. I heard him say, "She is not dead, but sleepeth."

Those near, who heard the words, laughed him to scorn. Where before there had been wailing and the beating of hands against the breast, now there were fingers upraised at what he said—that and a tapping of the forehead.

He spoke again, this time directly to my father. "Send them out, all of them. Away. Only the mother and you. Take me to her."

Father waited as my kinsfolk and neighbors crowded past him, astonished, through the gate, all the time babbling about the stranger—he should be bound, what new doctrine this, no good thing could come out of Nazareth, everyone knew the maiden was dead, had Jairus taken leave of his senses.

Silently father took my mother's hand and led the stranger into my chamber. I watched, hovering just above my bed, as he pulled back the sheet my mother had so lately drawn over my face. Then he lifted up his eyes—I thought first he looked at me, but saw at once he looked, far beyond—and prayed, saying, "Father, glorify thy name."

In that instant I felt a strong tugging downward—toward my body on the bed. For some reason I resisted but my strength could not withstand the embrace, as it were, of one larger than I.

Then I saw Jesus—so was he named—of Nazareth, take my hand lying still across the coverlet and he said, with great compassion—I can feel it yet—albeit a command: "Little one. I love you. Arise." I cannot answer why, only say that I obeyed and stood—no fever—well. My mother and my father stood still for a moment, until their stunned disbelief turned to joy. Then with glad tears both embraced me, clinging tight and almost smothering me with their kisses.

The stranger spoke only once more, before he left the room. "Give her something to eat."

That was near six years past.

(LIGHTS   FADE   on   JAIRUS' daughter.)

Who Is This Man?

(LIGHTS UP on Choric.)

CHORIC

Who is this man
          who stands and speaks?
          . . . who speaks
          as if by his word
                    the worlds are held together
          this man
                    whose call
                    commands
                    the elements?
          this man
                    who orders peace!
          this man whose word
                    calls forth life
                    and wholeness?
Who Is This Man?
          —thick fingers
          creased and calloused
                    by adze and plane
                    rasp and chisel
          gripped hard
                    to shape the timbers
                    of his trade?

. . . carpenter,
> bunched muscles
> rippling round
> beneath his tunic;
> builder—
wrenched from his bench
> to shape
> a new kingdom
with carpenter as king!
Who is this man?

Who Is This Man?
> —driven into desert
> > driven
> > biting sand
> > driven dry
> stinging
> burning sun
thirsty days
stretched across the dragging sunsets
> > forty
> days burning dry
> agony
> > driven into conflict
> across the landscape
> > of his spirit
> every breath of victory
> > near-smothered
> > by the tempter's wile
> > > reaching

into each human desire
to find the hook
of bondage
—driven wild across the sere battle-ground
of soul
and purpose
until the final triumph
of spirit over flesh!

Who Is This Man?
—who strikes down Lucifer
with a Holy Word
three times uttered
in blaze of clashing wills;
—who says to his underlings
demons—OUT!
. . . you may no longer live
in human habitation!
Who Is This Man?
—who commands the unclean spirits:

SILENCE! You may not speak,
you must keep my secret
that I am
whom you know me to be—
Son of God.

Silence!
you may not tell
this secret.

Who Is This Man?

               God-man
               man-God
        touching earth with spirit
        breathing heaven
        into clods—
               whose very word
               becomes flesh;
whose touch breath word
               grows into seeing
               into sound
               and into leaping limbs
        whose life
               gives birth
               to a new community
God-man
man-God
               touching earth with spirit
               breathing heaven
               into clods
               shaped by his hand from clay!

Who Is This Man?
        —who announces simply:
        the kingdom of God has now arrived
                      who says:
               it is here
               I am—bringing it!

Who Is This Man?

DECLARATION AND UNVEILING

Why Is the Mystery Locked Away?

(The tap-tap of a blind man's cane sounds faintly as the Choric begins, continuing unobtrusively. The first few Choric lines are repeated rapidly a few times in loud whispers as if many voices in a crowd are questioning their neighbors; then, finally, repeated once more in a single voice, normal tone.)

CHORIC

Who is he

    Who is this man?
    do you know
    have you heard the secret
    can you tell

        why is the mystery
        locked away?

   why are the acts of Jesus' power
   shadowed by his urgent pleas
   to those he healed—anon, anon—
   to tell no man

why are the demons
stern rebuked
by his command
and silenced with the words

"Hold thy peace,
You must not make me known?"

    why
    does voice from heaven
    speak twice
    the word
    "You are my son
    well-loved"?
  —and all the earth
  is bidden to be dumb?

  and why
  —a thousand thundering whys—
are those who follow
deaf and blind?
—so close upon his steps
but
stumbling still
in a dark cloud of ignorance
    numb to understanding
    to which he called them
    so they
    could share his way?

> *(Again, the whispering of the following lines, repeatedly, as if many voices in a crowd are questioning their neighbors.)*

who is he

    who is this man

      why is the mystery

      locked away?

        when will we know?

NARRATOR

"Is a lamp brought into the room to be put under a bucket or underneath the bed? Surely its place is on the lampstand! There is nothing hidden which is not meant to be made perfectly plain one day, and there are no secrets which are not meant one day to be common knowledge. If a man has ears, he should use them."

Bread and Blindness
Narration

NARRATORS
*(Two narrators begin this sequence, each
telling one of the feeding stories—somewhat
intermeshed—developing their own rhythms
"against" each other)*

The apostles returned to Jesus
and reported to him
every detail of what they had done and taught.
—"Now come along to some quiet place
by yourselves
and rest for awhile," said Jesus,
for there were people coming and going
so that they had not even time for meals.
They went off in the boat
to a quiet place
by themselves,
but a great many saw them go
and recognized them, and
people from all the towns
hurried around the shore on foot
and got there ahead of them.
When Jesus disembarked
he saw the large crowd

and his heart was touched with pity for them
because
they seemed to him
like sheep without a shepherd.
And he settled down to teach them
about many things.
As the day wore on,
his disciples came to him, and said:
—"We are right in the wilds here
and it is getting late.
Let them go now,
so that they can buy themselves
something to eat
from the farms and villages around here."

But Jesus replied,
—"You give them something to eat!" . . .
Give them bread—
                the hungry ones
                are waiting
give them bread . . .

                where in all
                this barren wilderness
                can we find . . .

. . . give ye them to eat.

                you call us
                to this lonely place
                to rest awhile
                because

> we ourselves could find
> no time to eat
> and now you say . . .

> . . .give them to eat.

> how
> from the emptiness
> which pangs us deep
> are we to find
> the gift of bread
> for those around us?

> —still you say
> give ye them to eat!

There was another occasion . . .
when a huge crowd had collected, and,
as they had no food,
Jesus called his disciples
and said to them—
"I feel sorry for all these people;
they have been with me now for three days
and have nothing to eat.
If I send them home unfed,
they will turn faint on the way;
some of them have come from a distance."
The disciples answered,
—"How can anyone provide all these
people with bread in this lonely place?"

(Pace begins to quicken slightly, anticipating the more urgent rhythms when the CHORIC begins. During the following sequence a number of participants—not CHORIC—could distribute bread to each other. Various patterns in pantomime could provide an effective backdrop to the words: 1. A movement of bodies choreographed with bread shared from the giver's hand to recipient's mouth—as each pair moves or meets down-stage. 2. Two pedestals—an actor on each and one below. The "below person" breaks bread and places it in the mouth of "pedestal person." Then, the persons in each pair reverse positions and repeat. 3. An actor representing Jesus, gives thanks, breaks bread into twelve pieces and distributes to the twelve who, in turn, circulate briefly in audience, distributing.)

—"How many loaves do you have?
Go have a look."
And when they had found out,
they told him,
"We have five loaves and two fishes." . . .

     . . . on the other occasion
     he asked and they said,
     "Seven."
     They had also a few small fishes.

Then Jesus directed the people
to sit down in groups on the green grass

so they sat down
by hundreds and by fifties.

NARRATORS IN UNISON

And taking the bread
        and the fish
                he looked up to heaven
                and blessed
                and broke the bread
                        and divided the fish
        and gave them to the disciples
        to distribute among the people.
Everybody ate
and was satisfied

NARRATORS SINGLY

Afterward
they collected
twelve baskets
full of pieces
of bread and fish
that were left over.

        . . . would you believe it?
        on the second occasion
        —after everyone ate to his heart's content—
        seven baskets were filled
        with the scraps that were left!

NARRATORS IN UNISON

. . . on both occasions
everyone
ate to their heart's content.

Willing to Eat the Crumbs

CHORIC

Everybody ate
the bread
        . . . for whom?
Everybody ate
        . . . for whom is this way?
Everybody ate
        . . . whose blind will see?
        whose lame will leap?
        whose desert will bring forth gushing springs?

Everybody ate
and was full!

            I want *you* to know—
                    the devils know
                    and shout my name

                    the Gentiles hear
                    and somehow
                    believe
                    that I have come
                    as bread
                    for them as well

I want *you* to understand
to *you* has been given
the secret
of the kingdom of God . . .

> . . . who can hear?
> who can understand?
> who can walk the Way of Holiness?
> . . . is there a word
> from the Lord?

> . . . be careful
> be careful how you listen . . .

PANTOMIME

(Simultaneous AUDIO Vignette)

LIGHTS UP on a table with several loaves of bread. A Pharisee is seated, with head covered, his prayer shawl around his shoulders, rocking back and forth as he utters an ancient prayer. To one side, at a smaller table, two or three Pharisees are washing their hands and arms—up to their elbows—making great ceremony of their ablutions. Special attention is given to the arm, up to the elbow. During the two or three minutes of the pantomime, the Pharisee at the table ceases his prayers, folds his shawl, and begins to break up the loaf—messily—so bits of bread fall to the floor. The Syro-Phoenician woman, who has been lurking in the background, stealthily but quickly comes forward each time a crust falls to the floor to pick it up and eat it. LIGHTS FADE TO HALF while action continues to a final freeze which is held momentarily—then LIGHTS OUT.

RECORDED AUDIO SEQUENCE
(Simultaneous Vignette)

NARRATOR

. . . and Jesus went into the territory of Tyre.

There he went into a house

and hoped to remain unrecognized.

That was impossible.

Almost immediately a woman of that area

came looking for him . . .

> *(Sound of flapping sandals, hurrying, then slowing, shuffling; then of clapping hands, as a greeting.)*

PHOENICIAN WOMAN

Ho, lord of this house.

> *(Clapping again. Footsteps.)*

MALE VOICE

Be at peace. What do you seek?

PHOENICIAN WOMAN

Him of Galilee. It is said, he is here.

MALE VOICE
(Hesitating.)

He is. He came just at dusk. He hoped to rest . . .

PHOENICIAN WOMAN

. . . I must see him. (*Sound of feet again.*)   My daughter, she is

sore distressed. . .

JESUS' VOICE

. . . you wish to see me?

PHOENICIAN WOMAN

The rabbi who loves, it is said . . .

MALE VOICE

. . . this is Jesus. Enter (*Sound of gate—opening and closing.*) I shall leave. (*Footsteps receding.*) Master, we shall sup soon.

PHOENICIAN WOMAN
(Distraught.)

Only a minute. Sir—my daughter—I knew we are not of the chosen—of Syria I am, a Phoenician, and my husband, a Roman. Our youngest child . . .

JESUS

What do you wish?

PHOENICIAN WOMAN

The daughter . . oh my lord . . .

> *(Sound of a muffled sob as she prostrates herself at Jesus' feet.)*

JESUS

Here. Rise. Take my hand. Your daughter. What do you wish?

PHOENICIAN WOMAN

She has a spirit—an unclean spirit. A vile voice which curses each step I take and tears her slender body through the night hours. Oh, sir, kind sir, it is said you—that the devils cannot stay when you give command. Could you come—come with me to— and speak the word? I beg you . . .

JESUS

I am of Israel . . . a Jew. I have come to the children of Abraham.

PHOENICIAN WOMAN

Oh my lord. This once—will you not—it is but a short way. I beg of you. Again and again she is torn . . .

JESUS

. . . is it right . . .

PHOENICIAN WOMAN

(Urgently.)

. . . for her body and spirit, I cry, peace. And you say you are come to Israel.

(Pause.)

What—what—of the Gentiles?

JESUS

Let the children be fed first. Is it right—you will understand the saying—is it right to take bread from the children and throw it to the dogs?

PHOENICIAN WOMAN

(The only sounds are her heavy breathing and occasional sound as she almost begins to speak, is silent, then begins again—slowly, with deep feeling.)

I understand, my lord. No it is not right to cast children's
bread to the dogs. But even the dogs will eat—they are willing
to eat the crumbs left by the children.

JESUS

Woman, for this saying your prayer is answered. Go in peace;
the evil spirit has left your daughter. She is whole.

*(AUDIO—CUT
LIGHTS—on pantomime—OUT.)*

Men as Trees Walking

CHORIC
> who is he
> who is this man?

> why is the mystery
> locked away?

> when will we know?
> when will we see?

NOTE: Mark records two healings of blind men. For dramatic purposes these stories have been merged somewhat in order to highlight the theme of sight and understanding which represents a major part of the bread sequence.

NARRATOR
And Jesus cometh to Bethsaida, and they bring a blind man to him, and besought him to touch him.

And he took the blind man by the hand, and led him out of the town; and when he had spit on his eyes, and put his hands upon him, he asked if he saw ought.

And he looked up and said,

BLIND MAN
I see men as trees walking . . . *(more quietly)* men as as trees

walking . . . *(very low)* trees walking—men as trees walking.

CHORIC

(I see)
men as trees walking

(they bring)
a blind man to him

(he asked)
do you see any thing?
anything?

NARRATOR

And Jesus said to the disciples:
   To you has been given
   the secret
   of the kingdom of God . . .
    . . . be careful how you listen . . .

    (The tap-tap of the blind man's cane rises,
    more urgently now—he has partial sight. A
    "buzzing" also ensues; whispered or low-
    voiced repetitions of following lines, in any
    order, from clusters in any location.)

CHORIC

*who is he
  who is this man

  why is the mystery
  locked away

when will we know?

five thousand men
are asking
who is this man
four thousand
shout
who is this man
why is the mystery
locked away
when will we know?

For whom is this way?
. . . whose blind will see?
whose lame will leap?
whose desert will bring forth
gushing springs?

For whom is the bread?
bread for the hungry
and more
twelve baskets seven
we are all filled
and there's more
twelve baskets seven
and there's more
twelve baskets seven
and there's more . . .

who is he
who is this man?

SINGLE VOICE
    whom do men
    say
    that I am?

CHORIC
(Echo.)
        that I am
        whom do men
        say
        that I am?
who is he
    who is this man
        some say
    John
        some say
    Elijah
        others say
    one of the prophets

 some are saying—
    (Shouts.)
    John
    Elijah
    one of the prophets

who is he
    who is this man
        —John

who is he
who is this man
    —Elijah

who is he
    who is this man
        —one of the prophets**

        *(Peak following a moderate crescendo—
        then total silence for the SINGLE VOICE.)*

SINGLE VOICE

I see men as trees walking.

        CHORIC

        *(The diaglogue parts in the following se-
        quence should be done by single voices.
        Choric may enter elsewhere as directed.
        Also. if controlled effectively. the low back-
        ground buzz of rhythmic questions continu-
        ing can enhance these lines and form a
        bridge to the next and final crescendo.)*

. . . as Jesus was leaving Jericho
with his disciples
and a large crowd,
they passed a blind beggar, Bartimaeus,
seated at the roadside.

    What is the sound?
    There is a crowd.

Yes, many people;
Jesus
walks this way.

 Of Nazareth?

The same.

 Ho,
 Jesus
 Jesus of Nazareth
 Son of David
 have mercy!

Be quiet.
He has no time.

 Jesus!
 have pity on me!

Silence.
He does not stop for beggars
Hold thy peace.

 —over here
 Son of David
 can you see me waiting?
 come to me with mercy—
 Ho Jesus!

Jesus stopped
and said,

call him

It's all right
stand up now
he's calling you

what

do you want me

to do

for you

Master
oh, Jesus
I want to see!

> *(CHORIC returns to lines beginning with single asterisk on page 120 up to double asterisk on page 123: this time moving the crescendo to a higher peak. Again there is sudden silence for SINGLE VOICE.)*

SINGLE VOICE

. . . And Whom

    Do You Say

    That I Am?

    (Appropriate pause. An electric bass guitar could come in with one final rhythmic beat sounding, for the last time, the question— who is this man?)

SIMON

      YOU are the *anointed one*

        Messiah Christ

CHORIC

(In dialogue form where necessary.)

To you has been given
the secret
of the kingdom of God

> . . . but tell no man
> it's still a secret.
> . . . and he began to teach them
> that the Son of man
> had to undergo great sufferings,
> and be rejected
> by the elders,
> chief priests,
> and doctors of the Law,
>> be put to death,
>> and rise again
>> three days afterwards.

. . . but Simon Peter
remonstrated with him

> He took Jesus by the arm,
> drew him to one side
> and said:
>> this cannot be!
>> the strong Messiah
>> Son of God
>> shall never suffer!
> nor will he die
> instead
> he shall reign for . . .
> *(Sharply!)*

Silence!
Hold your peace.

> *(Pause, then with deep compassion . . .)*

Oh, Simon Peter

you do not understand
are you still blind
are you still caught
by Satan's thoughts
of power
and the might of earthly kingdoms?

> Yes—
> I came
> to suffer—
> and to die;

for this
I was anointed!

> *(The tap-tap of the blind man's cane sounds
> suddenly, and he appears.)*

CHORIC
. . . men as trees walking
men as trees walking

Then Jesus put his hands
on the blind man's eyes
once more . . .

. . . and his sight
came into focus
and he recovered
        and saw everything
        sharp and clear.

Everything Sharp and Clear

Pantomime

(And the blind man breaks his cane, discarding the pieces. Here—to end this section—a delightful sequence could be choreographed where the first moments of perfect sight are experienced: gazing into distance—pointing, first one direction, then another; a modified jumping for joy; awareness of fingers—counting them, touching fingertips, etc.; awareness of a rose—holding it close to his eyes, peeking inside, etc.; awareness of a friend's face—touching it, looking closely at one or two features, looking into eyes, then in ecstasy embracing the friend, etc.; finally leaping and dancing for joy, shouting Glory to God, *dancing off-stage but with his exit interrupted by several stops to peer closely at a friend's face, then into the eyes, then embracing. As background to the choreography, a single, delicate voice could speak . . .)*

. . . and the blind man followed him on the way.

Then Will . . . Eyes . . . Be Opened
Narration

NARRATOR

Then will the eyes of the blind be opened
     and the ears of the deaf unstopped
Then will the lame leap like a deer,
     and the tongue of the dumb shout for joy.

Water will gush forth in the wilderness
     and streams in the desert
The burning sand will become a pool,
     the thirsty ground will be there . . .

And a highway will be there;
     it will be called the Way of Holiness
The unclean will not journey on it;
     it will be for those who walk in that Way . . .

We Have Seen His Power

CHORIC

We have seen his power
We have felt his touch
We have known his breath upon us
        but even though
        that day was glad
        which brought to us
        deliverance
            —there is more
            much more—
he has become our king
lord of our spirits
    Great Spirit
    Father God
    come in flesh
    as Son
        to make his kingdom
        here—
        among men
            and we—
    his early subjects
    sharply brought to faith
    by acts of Jesus-power,
    it is true

                                        —have gone beyond:
                              our vision reaches far beyond
                              the elements
                              from which we're made
                              and which we walk upon

. . . to his kingdom

                                             which

              by his Spirit
              is born
              and grows
              in hearts of those
                        who follow him
and make for him
a place
to rule
and finish

                   all his purpose.

Part II
THE KINGDOM WAY

THE GREATEST IS SERVANT OF ALL

A New Kingdom

(LIGHTS UP to HALF—SPOT UP on Choric. Trumpets—triple sequence.)

CHORIC

The King has come!
        Just like that
        Jesus of Nazareth
                walks out of the desert
                into Galilee
                and announces:
it's here
the kingdom of God
is here!
        (Trumpets—single sequence.)

. . . the kingdom of God
is here . . .
        like he had brought it
        with him
                as if he himself
                embodied
                the kingdom
                        he said

you must change
        your hearts
        and minds
        and believe the good news
it's here
the kingdom of God
is here

                you must change
                your hearts
                and minds . . .
                        hearts
                        and minds
                        which are convinced
                        the kingdom
                        was or will be
                you
                must
                change
                and
stop living in a noble history
where the only reality is
the past tense
                you
                must
                change
                and
stop living in the futile speculation
about a future
which is fully in the hand of God
        a future
        which is always beyond now

a future which
can never be
a present reality
              for if it becomes
              a present reality
              it is no longer future!
              you
              must
              change
              and
              (Trumpets—single sequence.)

believe the good news—
        it's here
        the kingdom of God
        is here
                    Now
        believe the good news
        God's kingdom is here
                    Now
. . . in me!
        your expectations
        have now come to birth
                your eschatology
                is realized
      . . . in me!
                the law
                is now fulfilled;
        he who was foreshadowed
                throughout your past

is
now
walking among you!

. . . I AM
is here . . .

(Trumpets—triple sequence.)

That
seems
to be
the message.
The king
has
come
and brought his kingdom
along.

The kingdom
came in
with Jesus
the kingdom
is
where Jesus is

you must change
your hearts
and minds
and believe the good news

*(Pause then LIGHTS   UP   SLOWLY to
FULL—drowning the SPOT.)*

. . . a new day has dawned . . .

        (A Mini-Choric ENTERS and establishes
        an antiphonal formation with the Choric
        group already present.)

          God's kingdom
          can't come now . . .

it's here

          . . . the Scriptures say:
          a root out of Jesse;
          Son of David
          a king . . .

this is he
. . . the king is here

          he has no throne

. . . his throne stands
in the hearts of men

          you are saying, then,
          God's kingdom
          is only a spiritual truth . . .

How right you are!
      and

          How wrong you are!
    . . . a spiritual truth, you say?
    of course,
    for the spirit of man
    calls for a king.
That's a spiritual truth—
and that's why
you find it difficult
to understand:

         your sight is
         so accustomed
         to the tangible material
         things around you!

. . . but,
only a spiritual truth?

         How wrong you are!

For in the order of things
the Father of all
breathed His spirit into flesh;
    that which cannot be seen
    is cloaked
    with that which our eyes behold;
        the spirit of our God
        has become
        incarnate!
             the kingdom
             will come

the kingdom has come

             will come

God's kingdom
comes to men
now—where they live
    in human need
    and fear
    —to change their lot
the kingdom is here

         we must work hard
         so his kingdom
         can come

we work
to do the will of God—
that is the hardest work
                to choose
to do
                the will of God
                        we must wait
                        until all the signs
                        are fulfilled
what kind of blindness
this
—or arrogance
        to wait for that
        which is already here
        among us?
                        we must wait
                        and watch
the kingdom of God
does not come
with observation
        —neither here
        nor there—
his kingdom is among you
        it's in your midst
        —it's that kind of kingdom!
                        the kingdom will come
The kingdom of God
is here!

Believe the good news:
                a new day has dawned!

Jesus talked often
> about his kingdom
> a different kind of kingdom
a kingdom
> where the king
>> —because he is king—
>> steps first on the path
>> his subjects must walk . . .
> where the king
> takes up his cross,
> where he suffers and . . .
>>> *But*
>>> a cross implies
>>> death . . .
whoever tries to save his life
shall lose it;
> a kingdom
>> where
>> servanthood always marks
>> those who follow the Christ . . .
>>> *But*
>>> servants
>>> must serve . . .
—anyone who wants to be great
will be servant of all
>>> servants
>>> must always think
>>> of others
>>> first . . .
—anyone who wants to be great
will be servant of all

        servants
        must give up
        their own desires . . .
—anyone who wants to be great
will be servant of all!

a kingdom

        where
        each must be like a child
        to walk in the way

        But
        children have no rights,
        no power.
. . . for of such is the kingdom of God
           they've done nothing
           of merit.
. . . for of such is the kingdom of God;
           they don't know how
           to keep the law;
           they're not at all
           traditional.
. . . for of such is the kingdom of God;
           they're humble
           amd unaspiring
           and unpretentious.
. . . for of such is the kingdom of God;
           they're not practical
           or realistic.
           Sometimes they seem

to be in a world of their own—
out of touch.
. . . for of such is the kingdom of God!

Jesus talked often
about his kingdom
a different kind of kingdom

—and
he lived that way!

*(The Choric cluster taking the negative view
goes into a huddle of heated gesticulation—
a pantomime of passionate reactions to the
recent statements, a leader possibly pointing
to each person in turn, the respondent
reflectng his views, then agreement and . . .)*

Give us a sign
Jesus—
how
do
we
know
that
what you say
is true?
. . . give us a sign.

And he sighed
deeply in his spirit:
why does this generation
seek after a sign . . .

                              . . . give us a sign
                              Jesus!

. . . the generation
that seeks after a sign is
evil
and adulterous;
having denied the covenant of faith,
they need a sign . . .

                              . . . a sign
                              Jesus;
                              just give us
                              a sign.

        the desire for a sign
        from heaven
                is a denial of faith
        the insistence on rational process
        alone
                is a denial of faith
        the refusal to leave the security of
        familiar traditions
                is a denial of faith
        the unwillingness
        to obey

                is a
                denial
                of faith

        and every denial of faith—
becomes a denial
of the kingdom of God

for faith
is the only sense
we can use
to perceive the kingdom of God;
    a faith that's alive
    is the only proof
    we are living
    in the kingdom of God;

a faith
that obeys . . .
    faith like a little child
    who trusts
    and follows . . .
        faith like a servant
        who commits all
        for the fulfillment and joy
        of another . . .
            faith that walks
            to the cross—
            knowing
            that new life grows
            from every dying!
. . . it's a different kind of kingdom . . .
        only a faith that lives
        is counted
        as righteousness;
            nothing else!

There is no place
for human pride
in the presence of God

      pride in
           things
      pride in
           dogma
      pride in
           power
      pride in
           fame
      pride in
           security
things, houses, and lands
     dogma, tradition and intellect
        power and position
           fame and prestige
   security and wealth with everything guaranteed
           this is why,
           to enter the kingdom
           —for some people—
           is so difficult.

There is no place
for human pride
in the presence of God . . .

           (. . . as echoes fading away.)

           . . . nor power
           position
           prestige
         . . . nor power
       position
       prestige

                    . . . nor power
                    position
                    prestige . . .

—in the kingdom of God
only a faith that lives
and obeys
is counted
as righteousness.

                    . . . not power
                    position
                    prestige . . .

Jesters Tell the Truth
Choric/Vignette

(Three jesters in clown costumes and fool's caps enter cavorting across the downstage area: leapfrogging, turning somersaults, cartwheeling, doing handstands, or headstands. The entire sequence—with the very brief dialogical interaction and the mini-Choric lines—is spoken against a background of physical acrobatics and restrained clowning. As many lines as possible are delivered from upside-down positions. Other Choric members may. be part of an active audience on stage or stage may be bare except for the three jesters.

FIRST JESTER
Hey, you want to hear an upside-down truth?

JESTERS TWO AND THREE
Yeah.

FIRST JESTER
(Standing on his head or hanging from a T-bar.)
If you want to live, you have to die.

> *(The others stop doing what they were doing momentarily—and gaze at him quizzically.)*

Or, if you want to die, just keep on living for yourself.

SECOND JESTER

I've got one too.

> *(Does his upside-down bit before he speaks.)*

If you want to be first, you've got to be last.

THIRD JESTER
> *(Gets into upside-down position.)*

Listen to this! If you want to be the biggest chief, you have to be servant of all.

> *(The three jesters form a mini-Choric. Each jester speaks only the lines found in one of the first three columns. All join to speak those lines found in column four. Where no directives are offered, the jesters may nonetheless continue their acrobatic cavorting so that each brief message "hangs in the air," punctuated by the physical movement.)*

If you want to live
you have to die—
and that's an
upside-down truth.
       Upside?

           down?

*(One does a quick handstand—grasped at
each ankle by partners.)*

                       It all depends
                       on which end
                       is up.

That's not really
an
upside-down truth; it's
kingdom truth . . .
                    It all depends
                    on how you stand.

To some . . .
      . . . living
      in Christ's kingdom . . .
                    . . . seems to be
                    upside down . . .

But it's really
right side up.
                    It all depends
                    on how you stand.

Try it and see
      —live for yourself
           —for fame
           —for riches
           —for power
                  . . . the end of that
                  is death. It has
                  to be; for all of that
                  is . . .

temp
         -o-
                  rary.
                           that is,
                           temporary

So it's better
         —far better—
                  to pronounce
                  a death sentence
                  on your desire
                  to be
                  for yourself
         —far better—
                           and live.

                  When you stop
                  living *for* yourself
                  then
         —at last—
your true being
can begin
to emerge,
the God-likeness in you
                  —at last—
                           and
                           that
                           is really living!

                  *(They jostle lightly with each other with
                  first jester always pushing himself into first
                  place. Finally, the second jester—exas-*

*perated—physically removes him and puts
him behind, saying . . .)*

Remember
—if you want to be first
you've got to be last
    of course
    if you prefer
    to be last,
    then . . .
all you need to do
is . . .

                struggle
      and
                fight
      and
                trample
      and
                climb
      and
                clutch all you can
      and
                as sure as
                we're standing here . . .

(All turn cartwheels to a new position.)

                . . . as sure as we were
                standing there
                —you'll be last!

That's what I said!
Or something like that
There's only one way—
in the kingdom of God
—to be chief

and that
        is to be

servant of all.

That's what I said
        That's
        a strange kingdom.

        (Pause.)

on second thought . . .
has it ever entered your mind
that this other kind
of kingdom
        is not

    so strange
        —is not
        so strange
        after all:

        After all,
        a king
        can decide . . .
                right or left
                yes or no
                if or whether.
        A king
        can decide . . .

(LIGHTS FADE to ONE-FOURTH.
Trumpet—single sequence.)

TOWNCRIER

Hear ye! Hear ye! The king has announced conditions to be met by all subjects. Hear ye! "Anyone who wishes to be a follower of mine must leave self behind; he must take up his cross and come with me. Whoever cares for his own safety is lost; but if a man will let himself be lost for my sake and for the Gospel, that man is safe. Hear ye! What does a man gain by winning the whole world at the cost of his true self?"

To Serve Is the Only Way

CHORIC

. . . the kingdom of God
is here
now
believe the good news
    repent
    turn around
    stand on your head—
            the
            "upside–down way
            of seeing things"
            has arrived!
Do you want to be first?
    —then be last;
    be servant of all!
    Do you want to live?
      —then die;
    stop living for yourself!
        What shall a man do to die?
        —just live for himself.
What shall a man do to live?
    —pronounce the death sentence
    on his desire to be
    for himself!

                    —not death to
                              the possible self;
                    —not death to
                              becoming that
                              which God intended;
                    —not death to
                              the self of worth
                              growing
                              into his likeness!

but DEATH to that desire
          to live
          only for oneself

                              —instead of
                              for others—

DEATH to that desire
          to grasp
          and cling to
          all that one is and has!

What does a man gain
          even
          if he wins the whole world
          at the cost of discovering his true self?
          Anyone who wishes to be a follower of mine
                    must leave the grasping self behind
                    must be willing to suffer and die
                    must come with me:
          . . . whoever clings to his life
          will lose it

But anyone who lets go,
who pries loose
his selfish grasp on things he calls his own
so my kingdom can grow;

> that one will discover
> what it means to live,
> to be fully alive
> > the
> > "upside–down way
> > of seeing things"
> > has arrived!

believe the good news

the kingdom of God
is here
now

—the kingdom
is
where Jesus is

> —among Jew or Gentile
> bond or free
> male or female;

—the kingdom
is
wherever people walk the Jesus way
> —from every nation
> east and west
> north and south;

—anyone—

anyone
who chooses
may come with me,
may be a follower of mine . . .

                   —whether young or old
                         black or white
                         primitive
                         or cultured

anyone
who wishes to be
a follower of mine . . .
          . . . must come
          with me

                   (must
                   come
                   with me)

The Son of Man himself
did not come to be served
          but to serve
          and to give his life
          to set many others free.
               the servant died
               on the way
               to exaltation

TO CHOOSE OR NOT TO CHOOSE
THE WAY

A Hard Choice

(LIGHTS at HALF.)

CHORIC

. . . that is why
those who cling to
        things
                        or
        dogma
                        or
        power
                        or
        fame
                        or
        security
have difficulty
                entering
                the kingdom of God
. . . it's a hard choice.

(LIGHTS OUT—ABRUPTLY.)

It Was a Sad Hour
Monologue

It was a sad hour.

I had gone, seeking him out, this teacher from Nazareth. So much of his teaching had come to my ears. A bit strange, perhaps. But all of it had a tone of authority.

I liked that; that meant we could understand each other.

What led me to seek him out? That is hard to say. I suppose— well, you see, I'm near my fortieth year. Well-schooled in the Law and the Prophets. Mother would have had me train as a lawyer—rabbinical law. But father was a merchant in spices, from the east. His trade was growing; he had become very wealthy. He needed my help to deal with the caravans.

Suddenly, he was gone—barely a score of years more than I am this day. And his wealth was mine.

Three years have passed. Good years. Mother and my sister both have sumptuous houses and dress in the finest of silk and linen. There are servants—servants for the morning and servants for the evening.

My own houses—one in Jerusalem, the other at the sea—are, either one, large enough to house a centurion and his troops.

My trade has doubled. I am a ruler in the synagogue. Even my friends bow when I pass.

But, as I said, my years are nigh twoscore. And I have no wants. Yet within me there lies a restlessness, a nameless hunger, a fear whose shape I cannot form in words.

Each time I heard something about the words of this teacher, I felt a strange tugging at my heart. As if what he was saying would satisfy this hunger, this reaching for something more, when so much—so much lay under the beckoning call of my little little finger.

So I purposed to meet him. Of course I could not bring him to the house; I had heard he had with him crude fisher-folk. I therefore summoned a servant with command that when the teacher came near he would haste to tell me.

Thus it was, one day, I met him in the way and knelt before him.

I remember yet the hot sun pressing down, the curious onlookers, the dusty road, his sandal—he had a torn sandal, one thong was rent—and the cockleburrs stuck fast on the hem of his garment.

I knelt and said, "Good Master, what must I do to inherit eternal life?" Even today, I'm not certain of all that lay within those words. Perhaps a wish that some great good deed would make more sure my riches for the morrow. Or that, when I should be gathered to my fathers, I'd hear "Well done." But deeper still—of this I fear almost to speak, for it strikes my very breath away—a lurking fright that somewhere I had missed the way of righteousness given by Jehovah to our father Abraham and thus, that all I called my own was only straw. Further, that this lack was the spring from which bubbled each day my nameless hunger.

All this and more was clutching at my throat when I spoke the words—and held me in their vise until I heard his voice cut through my reverie.

"Why callest thou me good? There is none good but one, that is God."

I could not answer. It had seemed only right to call him "good." And even when he remonstrated I could not rid my heart of some strange certainty that I had been right to call him good.

"You know the commandments," he said.

I thought, how did he know that I knew the law? Had my name come to his ears? How did he know the years I had spent reciting from the Torah? "Do not commit adultery. Do not kill. Do not steal. Do not bear false witness. Defraud not. Honor the father and mother."

How did he know? I answered him. I spoke only truth. "These have I kept, O Master, from my youth." And from my heart came loud a soundless cry—tell me, great teacher, some other commandment, some other law which, having kept, I will find my hunger stilled.

I looked full at him. It seemed almost as if he heard my silent supplication. For when he looked at me I could read compassion, love and deep desire writ large across the gentle lines upon his face. And I waited—kneeling there in the dusty road, unmindful of the crowd, having eyes only for him who looked upon me there and heard my hunger, of that I'm sure.

Then he spoke. To this day I cannot escape his words. Like a knife, gently but surely, probing deep into my being his words cut through all I held dear and, in an instant, I knew that I had sought all the wrong food for my hunger. And that I would feel this hunger until I died unless I would heed the signpost marked in pain across my heart that day.

"One thing thou lackest: go thy way, sell whatsoever thou hast, and give to the poor, and thou shalt have treasure in heaven: and come, take up the cross, and follow me."

That was a sad hour, as I went away.

Part III
THE TEMPLE FOR ALL NATIONS

LATER CONFLICT—JESUS AND THE PHARISEES

The Temple Cleansed
Vignette

(A meeting of some Pharisees. The setting for this vignette may be simple—no more than a table and several chairs.)

(LIGHTS FULL or a SPOT on the area.)

JESHUAH
(Speaking with dignity and deliberateness; at the same time exercising obvious control over his passionate feelings.)

I am Jeshuah—known to most of you—elder of the chief priests called to serve in the temple of the Blessed One; of the sons of Eleazer; in the first course, according to our father Aaron; governor of the sanctuary. We have come together this day to take counsel: what shall be done with Jesus of Nazareth—*(Murmuring assent.)*—whose presence here in David's city bodes great ill, save we act to silence this scourge. It lacks but two days before Passover . . .
(More murmuring. Jeshuah holds up his hand for control.)

. . . before the sun sets to herald the Sabbath, we must see to it—somehow—that his feet do not walk our streets, that his presence among us does not give rise to further displays by the rabble . . .

*(Suddenly, at the memory of what Jachin
has told him, Jeshuah's fury shows itself in a
curled lip, nearly clenched teeth and steely
tone.)*

. . . Jachin, say to the assembly what your eyes witnessed on
the first day of this week. Mark well his words and you will
see . . . never mind; Jachin, to the point, without delay, we
have much to do this day. Say on.

JACHIN

*(A bit of a long-winded bumbler. Excitable.
Scatterbrained. The kind about which one
wonders—how did they get into a position of
responsibility?)*

The sun was warm but not yet high when I left by the east
gate—after my morning course at the temple—for Bethany
where a kinsmen lies ill . . .

JESHUAH

(Impatient, but controlled.)

. . . to the point . . .

JACHIN

. . . as I came through the gate I saw in the valley before me a
crowd, as if it were already the ninth hour and in the center,
upon the foal of an ass, the prophet of . . .

JESHUAH

(Steel in his voice.)

. . . .guard thy words. He who is called by some, a prophet.
Go on.

JACHIN

. . . . and all around him a multitude that went before and
that followed, waving branches and shouting—Hosanna,

Blessed is he that cometh in the name of the Lord. Hosanna in the highest. And others—Blessed be the coming kingdom of our Father David, He who comes in the name of the Lord. And many spread their garments in the way. It was he, the one from Nazareth . . .

JESHUAH

. . . where went he then . . .

JACHIN

I stepped aside and stood while he, while the multitude went by . . .

(Looks up and sees Jeshuah's impatience.)

. . . through the gate nearest the temple . . .

JESHUAH

(Interrupting.)

. . . enough. He was seen there after the noon sacrifice. A rabble around him—hanging on every word. Then he left. On the second day, the day before yesterday . . . Amariah, speak your witness. I will add betimes. We both were there . . .

AMARIAH

(Cool, credible; picking up on a nod from Jeshuah.)

I was coming from my chamber above—by the south stairs—when I heard loud shouting in the Court of the Gentiles . . .

JESHUAH

. . . and I, with the lord of the treasury, had just finished settling a dispute between two of the money changers . . .

AMARIAH

. . . I hurried over, pushed my way through the crowd to see—there, him of Nazareth, in the midst of the sellers and the money changers, unbinding the feet of doves so they flew away, wrenching the tethers of kids loose from their rings in the floor and walking from one to the other, full circle, tipping tables, tumbling chairs until all were unseated and scrambling for farthing coins and bleating kids alike . . .

(A few cover their amusement at the graphic picture with hands and turned heads.)

JESHUAH
(Roaring.)
. . . silence in the assembly! Well might we chuckle at the games of this imposter if he were not threatening our very livelihood.

(Quietly to Amariah.)
. . . you heard him speak?

AMARIAH
. . . yes, all the time saying. "Out, away from here, defilers of the house of God. Ye who buy and sell. Is it not written, My house shall be called a house of prayer for all nations . . ."

JESHUAH
(Ice cold.)
. . . with my own ears. I heard him say, "Ye have made it a den of thieves."

(A murmur arises and voices cry out.)
How dare he speak thus?
Blasphemer!
The temple is not his!
He is a subverter of the old order!
He would open wide our temple to the Gentiles!
He is against Caesar!
Away with him!
He himself will not pay taxes!
(Louder than others.) By what authority does he these things?

JESHUAH

That is the question we asked of him the day after—yesterday
it was . . .

GERSHON

. . . he came again?

JESHUAH

He came again, no whit more humble as he walked through
the court to see, no doubt, whether the . . .

> *(Commotion at the door. A man pushes past
> the page, rushes over, bows, kneels . . .)*

. . . what meaneth this?

> *(Looks at door, at page who responds with a
> gesture of helplessness, then scathingly at
> the intruder.)*

Have you no respect for a closed door—for the privacy of
chief priests and scribes . . .

INTRUDER

> *(Breathless.)*

. . . your pardon. A thousand pardons. I have a message my
heart tells me your ears—if I be not mistaken—would pay
gold to hear. Could we speak, in private?

JESHUAH

> *(Pauses, considering; then beckons.)*

Come hither. I cannot leave. Tell me here.

> *(They huddle, earnestly—then break. But
> Jeshuah grasps his cloak brings him back
> with a whispered question—what is his
> name?—and a quickly whispered response.
> The other steps aside. JESHUAH—barely in
> control.)*

Here. Do not leave. Stand by me.

(JESHUAH turns, livid.)
We have a messenger—if he speaks truth—with a word from one of the motley hangers-on of this—prophet from Nazareth. Zerah here of Bethany. Say on. But take heed that thou sayest with exactness the words this Judas told thee.

ZERAH

He is my kinsman. Judas Iscariot. We had often close intercourse until—until he left to follow the teacher from Nazareth. He is keeper of the purse. Since, we have scarce crossed paths—until today—he sought me out—scarce an hour ago—sore distraught—he said the Master—*(Murmurs.)*—so he called him—had said—in truth, he told his disciples these selfsame words that *he was Messiah (Louder murmurings.)* . . .

JESHUAH
(Sharply.)
. . . give him leave to finish.

ZERAH

. . . and that—these are the words of Judas—before the Blessed One I swear by heaven . . .

JESHUAH
(Coldly.)
. . . go on . . .

ZERAH

. . . on this very day, since sun-up, as they were leaving . . .

JESHUAH

. . . they?

ZERAH

... Jesus and his disciples—as they were leaving the temple—
one of the twelve in marvel called out the cubits of the hewn
stones and thus remarked about the grandeur of this . . .

JESHUAH

. . . finish . . .

ZERAH

... the grandeur of this temple. And Jesus said, I swear by
heaven . . .

(Glances nervously at JESHUAH.)

. . .he said. Seest thou these great buildings? I tell you, there
shall not be left one stone upon the other, that shall not be
thrown down . . .

*(Pandemonium breaks loose with all rising
and speaking at once. One pushes to the
fore, demanding JESHUAH'S attention
but going on before he is given leave to
speak . . .)*

SHELEMOTH

. . . I heard him too . . .

JESHUAH

. . . when? These words?

SHELEMOTH

. . . not these words. Words like. Not this day. Two days ago.
After he broke apart the tables of the money changers . . .

JESHUAH

. . . then is when we spoke to him and asked him by what authority he did these things. *(Angrily.)* And he played games
with us—asked whether John's baptism was from heaven or

of men. If we answered, he would tell us by whose authority he did these things. It was not safe for us to answer—with the rabble crowding round.

SHELEMOTH

. . . later, I heard him.

JESHUAH

Later? We left him then and he walked away.

SHELEMOTH

I know. We watched you. I with Gershon here heard you speak. And heard him answer. Saw you turn; we followed him to ask another question . . .

JESHUAH

. . . another question?

SHELEMOTH

Yes, a sign. Would he give us a sign to prove he had authority?

JESHUAH

. . . and he said?

SHELEMOTH

Destroy this temple and in three days I will raise it up.

JESHUAH
(Roaring.)

He said?—what?

SHELEMOTH

This is my sign. Destroy this temple and in three days I will raise it up.

JESHUAH

Madman. He will tear apart the fabric of our social order.

AMARIAH

They agree. The testimony of Shelemoth. The word of Zerah, from Judas.

VOICE

Can we trust this word of Judas. Is it true?

JESHUAH

(Building from steely slowness to a passionate outburst.)

It agrees. But true or not, it is good enough as a witness against this—this insurrectionist. He is not satisfied to lay waste our traditions, to attack our Sabbath, to make fools of our learned scholars. Now he would strike at the center of our life—our temple—and with its fall plot further to destroy the forms which have taken our fathers centuries to build.

(LIGHTS OUT—ABRUPTLY.)

Tenants in the Vineyard
Narration

*(Here a cast or choric—alternative to Nar-
rator—could use choreographed movement
to enhance the lines.)*

(LIGHTS—SPOT UP.)

NARRATOR
Before the chief priests and scribes and elders went away
Jesus began to speak to them in parables:
> A man
> once planted a vineyard;
> put a wall around it,
> hewed out a winepress
> and built a watchtower.

Then
he let it out to vine-growers
and went abroad.
> At the end of vintage season
> he sent a servant
> to the tenants
>> to collect from them
>> his share
>> of the season's harvest.

                                   But
                                   they took
                                   that servant,
                                   thrashed him
                                   and
                                   sent him away
                                   empty–handed.
              The owner tried again;
              he sent another servant.
              This one
              they beat about the head
              and treated outrageously.
So he sent another;
that one they killed.
                   He sent many others—
                   some they beat up;
                   others they killed.
At last, he had one man left
to send;
his own son
who was very dear to him.
                   They will surely respect my son,
                   he said to himself.
                   But the tenants said to one another,
                   "This is the heir; come,
                   let us kill him,
                   and the property will be ours."
                                   So they seized
                                   him
                                   and killed him

   and threw

   his body

   out

   of the vineyard.

  What will the owner

  of the vineyard

  do?

He will come

and put the tenants to death

and turn the vineyard over to others!

   Can it be,

   Jesus asked,

   that

   you

   have never read

   this text:

 the stone which the builders rejected

 has become

 the main cornerstone.

  This the Lord's doing,

  and it is wonderful

  in our eyes!

Then they began to look for ways to get their hands on him.
For the chief priests and the scribes and the elders knew
perfectly well that he had aimed this parable at them. But
they were afraid of reactions from the people. So they left him
alone, this time, and went away.

(SPOT FADES.)

NO CURTAIN NOW

Rent in Twain

(LIGHTS UP to ONE-HALF.)

CHORIC

And
sitting down
they watched him
there

    and they that passed by
    railed on him,
    wagging their heads,
    and saying, ah,
        thou
        that
        destroyest
        the temple
    and buildest it
    in three days
        save
        thyself;
        come down
        from
        the cross

Likewise also
the chief priests mocking
said among themselves
with the scribes:
     He saved others
     himself he cannot save;
Let Christ the King of Israel
descend now from the cross
that we may see
and believe.
     (LIGHTS FADE to one-fourth.)

And at the ninth hour
     Jesus cried with a loud voice:
          My God,
          my God
          why hast thou
          forsaken me?
. . . and gave up his spirit.

     (Pause—then SUDDENLY and simul-
     taneously with LIGHTS UP to FULL. . .)

And
the veil in the temple
     was rent in twain
          rent in twain
          rent in twain
     from the top to the bottom
     it was rent in twain
the veil in the temple

from the top to the bottom
was rent in twain

> *(LIGHTS begin SLOW FADE as the voices
> taper until LIGHTS OUT. Tapering car-
> ried out by dropping out one or two voices
> with each repetition and increasing softness
> until only one voice is barely heard . . .
> NOTE: speed of tapering and number of
> repetitions totally at the director's discre-
> tion.)*

veil in the temple
    rent in twain
veil in the temple
    rent in twain
veil in the temple
    rent in twain
veil in the temple
    rent in twain
veil in the temple
    rent in twain

(LIGHTS OUT.)

veil in the temple
    rent in twain

It Was a Bad Day
Monologue

ROMAN CENTURION

(The mood throughout is generally contemplative with bursts of passion punctuating the painful remembering, breaking through the disciplined military stance.)

. . . blood and guts . . .
it was a bad day
on that stinking hill . . .
we had drawn lots—
the other centurions and I
—for the crucifixion detail;
our last duty
before setting sail for Rome
—and home;
two years assigned
to the command of Pontius Pilate;
a whole legion,
our cohort at the palace;
my century often
his personal guard
when he sat in judgment;

     for our cohort
     that included
     executions.
it was a bad day . . .
     a dozen of us
     saw to
     the condemned;
        the nailing,
     that never takes long.
the others in my company
     I had assigned
     to crowd–control . . .
. . . a jostling mass
     motley
     rabble mixed with Pharisees
     pious and profane
     silent ones and raucous
     jeering
     taunting multitude
        and everywhere
        dogs
     sniffing curs
     yelping underfoot
        boisterous youth
        pelting
        the condemned
        with pebbles and
        clumps of mud
     an unruly crowd
     my men had their hands full.

. . . some priests from the temple
and scribes
          stepping carefully around
          the smoking refuse
          lifting their righteous skirts
                    as they picked
                    their path
                    to stand and
                    watch men die . . .
. . . one
whom they had brought to Pilate;
                              —on that day I hated.
          it was a bad day
          I was thinking
          a bad day
                    I wished then
                    I had never left Rome
          or
                    that this hour
                    had been held dangling
                    somehow
                    until I had gone back to Rome
. . . then . . .
          he looked at me
          and said:
          Father, forgive them,
          they know not what they do.
                    He looked at me
                    —I swear
                    by Jupiter—

      he looked full upon me
             his words
             drove judgment
             piercing
             into my heart
but
in the same instant
he looked upon me
      love and forgiveness
and I knew
that when he answered Caiaphas—
      I had heard the High Priest ask
             Art thou the Christ
             Son of the Blessed?
             and the answer also I heard:
      I am
—I knew that
when he answered Caiaphas
the words were true
                  and
                  at the cross
             with darkness all around
             and brutal hypocrisy
             hanging in the air
             and his forgiveness
             reaching me warm
      I could only
      step close
      in wonder and say
      —there was no doubt—
Truly this man was the Son of God.

FINALE – THE SERVANT DIED ON THE WAY TO EXALTATION

Marcus
Monologue

I heard the centurion speak those words—Son of God—and I trembled. For the same words had grown in my heart during the months before he came again, this last time, to Jerusalem. An awe crept into my being and claimed many of my waking hours—not so much because in his dying hour Jesus had called forth a word of faith from this Roman, as that God had found a way to come to men.

The scattered scratchings I was making—to help my mind reclaim again the passing thoughts—grew to a torrent. Tumbling phrases, remembered images, a pithy saying, a jumble of sentences from this disciple or that, a witness to the acts of power upon a crippled body, his teachings on the way of giving all as salvation, the touch of love he gave to each one who crossed his path.

All of this and more was etched upon me.

How—how can I tell in words alone, the helpless wonder at his certain path? The bursting of my spirit with joy and fear as I saw he brought a new way for men to walk. The rending pain I felt to see him rudely bound, struck by the staves of rabble and dragged to a place of hollow judgment, then before the third hour racked upon a frame reserved for the base and low, murderers. Where should have hung—oh my

God, forgive—those who called for his blood, who snatched his life away

Or how can I tell the strange peace which whelmed me even as I watched—amidst all the turmoil in my heart of hate and despair—peace which held a quiet knowing that this horrendous crime against him was somehow a part of the way he chose to walk.

I remember, I started at the thought—the way he chose to walk. From that moment, I knew there would be other wonders. For as the Roman said, full in my hearing unmindful of the restless crowd, lost in his own awakening: truly this man was the Son of God!

After the Cross
Narration

NARRATOR

As soon as the Sabbath was over, Mary the Magdalene and Mary mother of James and Salome bought aromatic oils so they could anoint the body of Christ. Hurrying to the tomb very early on the Sunday morning, just as the sun was rising, they wondered among themselves who would roll back the entry stone. But when they arrived they found the huge stone already rolled back. Inside on the right sat a young man wearing a white robe. They were dumbfounded.

He said to them, "Don't be afraid. You are looking for Jesus of Nazareth who was crucified. He has risen, He is not here. See, there is the place where they had laid him."

"Go now and tell his disciples. Give this message to Peter: 'He will go on before you into Galilee. You will see him there just as he told you.' "

In fright they left the tomb and ran away. They said nothing to anyone, for they were too filled with fear!

Whose Way Leads Through a Tomb

CHORIC

Who is this man

        God–man
        man–God

    touching earth with spirit
    breathing heaven
    into clods

        whose very word
        becomes flesh

whose touch breath word

        grows into leaping limbs

    what new order this
    in which

        forms give way
        to need

    and

        worth of person
        shatters dogma?

        who
        is
        this man

bursting the old wineskins

      of tradition
      the holy vessels of centuries
with his new wine
      the wine of freedom
      spirit rending flesh
      with kingdom newness
splitting the shapes
      of predictability
tearing apart the fabric
      of religious respectability
splintering the venerable frames
      of suitability

spirit *dunamis*
    EXPLODING
      from the inner core
      of Godness
      in the flesh

who is this man

      God–man
      man–God
    whose way
    leads through a tomb
      whom life
      could not contain
      whom the grave
      could not hold

spirit *dunamis*
>> EXPLODING
>>>> from the inner core
>>>> of Godness
>>>> in the flesh
a new day
>>>> rolling back the darkness
a new kingdom
>>>> sweeping crumbling forms into the dust
a new king
>>>> ruling as Lord of all;
>> crumbling dynasties
>>>> clawing for lost power
>>>> fading
>>>>> like fog
>>>> —rolled back by heat
>>>>> of morning sun

(Collage of sound—SUB-VOCE.)

into the dust into the dust into the dust into the dust

*(LIGHTS FADE SLOWLY to match the
receding collage, then—LIGHTS
UP FULL.)*

There Is a Way — to Exaltation

*(A brief trumpet sequence, in reveille-style,
or a few bars from a familiar hymn—only
enough to introduce the theme in preparation for the ending.)*

CHORIC

There is a way . . .

    marked across the geography of time

      . . a torturous way

      . . a joyful way

               at times

          dropping into the valleys of everyday

          mortality;

               at the same time

          transcending body and place,

          and wending

          a heady path

          past the peaks of eternal reality

    glistening

          (in)

evening's promise

          (of)

a new day

                  . . . a way

which now and then

is clearly seen
or suddenly hid from view
now sharply shaped
each rocky detail
and
twisting form
stark—
then (and most often)
both feet and path
lost in an earthy haze
so that each step—
made firmly
—must be made
in faith.
. . . a way
—marked by one
who has walked it
in
both directions—

*(A change of pace and setting which can be
signaled choreographically, or otherwise.)*

Let this mind be
in you
which was also
in Christ Jesus
who,
though the divine nature
was his from the first,
did not prize his equality with God
a thing to be grasped . . .

                              this is the way
      but,
      stripped himself
      of all privilege,
      literally
      emptied himself . . .
                              this is the way
            then,
            taking for himself
            the form of a servant,
            he assumed the very nature of a slave
            and became mortal man . . .
                              this is the way
        revealed then,
        in human likeness
        and born in the flesh,
        he humbled himself . . .
                              this is the way
. . . he humbled himself
and accepted death,
even death on a cross . . .
                        the servant died
                        on the way!
Because of all this
        God has highly exalted him
                (Trumpets—single sequence.)
        and has given him
        a name
        above all names
                glory
                (Trumpets—double sequence.)

a name
above all names
glory
hallelujah
(Trumpets—triple sequence.)
that,
at the name of Jesus

Son of Man
Messiah Christ
Son of God
I Am

at the name of Jesus
every knee shall bow
every knee in heaven
every knee on earth
every knee under the earth
shall bow
and every tongue confess that . . .

*(Trumpets—triple sequence, as Choric
members and entire cast cluster with
upraised arms and conclude in a crescendo
joining voices and trumpets.)*

. . . Jesus Christ is Lord
Jesus Christ is Lord
Jesus Christ is Lord
to
the glory
of God
the Father

(Trumpets—triple sequence.)

(LIGHTS OUT—ABRUPTLY
then almost immediately
(LIGHTS FADE IN to silhouette the
Choric.)

(Final lines in quiet awe!)

. . . every knee shall bow
and every tongue confess
to
the glory
of God
the Father . . .

JESUS CHRIST IS LORD!

(LIGHTS OUT.)

EPILOGUE

Epilogue

The writing of *To Walk in the Way* became, for me, a totally unexpected pilgrimage.

Ill-equipped as well as unprepared for an arduous journey, I was nonetheless captivated by the beckoning hand of a fellow-writer who had discerned and walked in the way that Jesus taught. From my first honest immersion in his message, John Mark's style and his quiet certainties laid claim on my attention and finally on my response, and would not let me go. Through all my vigorous protestations that I was only writing dramatic interpretations of Jesus' teaching and of historical events, that claim held me fast until, like Mark it seemed, I too had caught a glimpse of glory from the mountain. From that moment forward there was no thought of turning back.

No words better describe the course of my humbled path than Willard Swartley's profound and exciting structural analysis of Mark's Gospel—found in his companion volume, *Mark: The Way for All Nations.* From the wanderings of Israel on their way to Canaan, he lifts the focal points: *sea, mountain, wilderness, way,* and finally a *temple* for all nations. In this outline which John Mark uses I found the way of discipleship clearly marked with its salient features starkly framed—commitment and following, suffering and ecstasy, wavering doubt and firm faith, agonizing conflict and quiet victory.

These metaphors became strangely intermixed. Sometimes in sequence, other times layered one upon the other—each was an entity in itself yet at the same time a component of all the others. A birthing by the *sea,* struggle in the *wilderness,* suffering on the *way,* glory from the *mountain,* and a new *temple* became a medley of figures—singular and merging—during my search for the reality of which John Mark wrote. Ultimately, for me, *way* encompassed all of the others.

I have been changed. I can no longer speak glibly of following Christ. For through the window of insight which revealed the way of Christ, I caught a glimpse of other truth—my lurking unwillingness to walk truly in that way, my ever-ready tendency to search elsewhere for an easier path, my hope that each step of his long road through suffering and death need not be mine.

During the months of my writing I trembled often at the awesome sense of Presence. I wept, trying to hide my face from the sight of my own heart. I cringed before the crests of insight which swept as waves across my being. For each revelation assaulted my will afresh until weariness with the constant choosing seemed to overwhelm my searching spirit.

There was no surcease. I had not before known truth to be so relentless. But in those days I was pilloried—as it were—before a mirror, face-to-face with truth splintered and distorted by my own misshapen image which often filled the glass.

Despair and awe wrenched me to and fro into exhaustion. But always, when it seemed no shred of strength was left to go on, I would look up and some startling light of glory from the mount would split my overcast sky with hope of my becoming and I could go on.

A pilgrimage, in fact, shaped like none before. (And I pray like none to come!)

First, there was *the sea*—that primal element from which beginnings thrust their shape into consciousness. Like the Israelites pursued by the Egyptians I felt panic as I saw the sea.

Behind me thundered the press of forces I could not withstand. Before me lay what looked like a watery grave. Yet, in that hopeless moment when only helplessness was sure, there came the wind of God as I stepped into the fearsome waters and walked—walled by mighty power—through my expected tomb into a new day beyond. Like Abraham, who resolutely moved out from the womb of his familial security, I found that each new warm home of the familiar must be left behind by a new birthing. And that this is living.

Therein lay the struggle—a struggle in *the wilderness*. Always a giving up of the cherished securities to which our time-bound hearts cling. Always a thrusting from the womb into the uncertainties of another new world. Always the bleak desert stretching away toward an empty horizon which only confirmed my utter aloneness in the choosing.

It was then I saw that choice is both bountiful gift and mother of conflict.

To choose! What should I choose? The glinting of gold which promises creaturely comfort, freedom from want, and a caging of that elusive animal—happiness?

Or should it be the scepter, symbol of lordship, power over the choices of others?

Perhaps fame. The glory of a name well-known, before which the nameless masses bow, bent by ignorance of their own birthright and their fawning thoughtless praise of temporary success.

Why not all three? Wealth, power, and fame caught up in one and held close to the beating heart, cherished until the last silence which signals exit from time and space—signals the foolish uselessness of that which, by its nature, is locked into our mortality.

What should I choose? There is where the battle of my will is always fought. Chained to a wilderness, alone. Deep in a Gethsemane from which the only path leads to a dying— unless I choose the temporary. Impaled on the vision of John

Mark so graphically outlined. Caught fast by his own commitment wherein vision and way were becoming one.

Choice, the highest gift to man! That gift, which can open all the doors to fulfillment of his inner self, his being made in God's image. Or can lead him to a thousand deaths—once breath is gone—withering final destruction of all the latent dimensions of his being; and that always within the consciousness of what might have been; and that sadly always in the presence of the gnawing hungers—never stilled nor filled—for wealth, for power, for fame; and that forever with the knowledge there can never be a filling, for that world of time and things will have passed away.

So what if I choose *his way*—knowing yet not knowing what lies before? Knowing it is not a lazy woodland stroll with soft moss gently underfoot. Not knowing how many times it will seem harsh beyond the bearing. Knowing it is clearly marked. Not knowing how much my earthly vision fogs the way and makes each footfall a trembling act of faith. Knowing there is a summit lost in the light. Not knowing to what dizzy heights that final torturous path will lead. Knowing that his glory is gifted to me through faith-eyes which claim the vision of his image formed in me. Not knowing how much my dust-bound blindness will war at every turn against my spirit's reach toward our Father's kingdom framed in love.

It was a blindness which puzzled and angered and bound my feet with hesitation. Surely with one touch of glory the blind eyes should be forever opened. But instead, for me, there was too often the darkness of eyes which could not, would not see. Eyes tuned to the glitter of baubles, thus dull to the hidden sheen of the eternal. Eyes wide open to man's countless conjecturings, thus closed too often to eternal truth. So my days of search were scarred by gropings, stumblings, frequent fallings until I despaired that clear sight or a certain footing could be mine again.

Then, when my spirit had worn itself down once more to quiet, would come those wonderful shattering glimpses of glory in *the mountain*—and the path lay clear before me.

When the stunned joy gave way to thought, I found a question surging into words—what is that glory?—and an answer shaped in the same instant.

Heavenly glory? Yes. The glory of the Infinite One. Without a doubt. But also—I began to see—the glory that can be mine. The glory which I bring to Him when I am all I'm made to be. The glory which I reflect when I let His nature—Love which gives, infinitely—come alive and shape my living. I catch a fuller view of the path then, not so much of suffering and death as rather a path of choosing to be what He has made me to be—what He can help me to become. And that a suffering and a dying are only concomitants of this way.

I saw the choice outlined sparely in the shape of incarnation: Not to get but to give! Not to cling to and grasp but to give up! Not to be served but to serve! Not to search first and always for my own filling but to become bread for another's hunger!

Blinding swelling encompassing burst of glory from the mountain and I knew in that instant I was seeing not only the glory of the Infinite One but the puzzling joyous glory of my becoming like Him—in His image—through His grace and power. That this measure of Himself could be seen in a human body, that choosing to walk in His path could bring forth His likeness in me dazzled every sense and I sat numb.

In that moment as never before I beheld the path I must walk, wanted to walk. And I realized that giving up my will is not the demand of a divine autocrat but rather a gentle loving instruction from the Father of my spirit—Maker of the universe, infinite Wisdom, encompassing Love—on how to enjoy infinite wealth, on how truly to experience supremacy and power, on how to be fulfilled in glory.

I saw too the way marked clearly by my elder brother, Jesus, who clothed his glory in humanity, who covered his power with mortality, who gave up his supremacy for an ultimate servanthood. In that setting of servanthood, he showed how Love gives itself fully.

I also knew that all I may become is already seeded in me. My spirit, brought to life by my Father's quickening breath, has in it the throbbing of his love and the stretching of his infinity. Limited in me, of course, by time—a span of years called a single lifetime; and by space—body and geography. But there comes a day when my fullness—or as well said, his fullness in me—will be no longer boundaried and I shall be like him for I shall see him as he truly is!

Finally, I have found *a new temple*. From another writer's record, I remembered what Jesus said to the wanton Samaritan beauty at Jacob's well.

"You think worship is carried out in this mountain or that? Neither. Those truly worship whose spirits bow to Spirit-God in truth."

I began to discover the old structures were laid waste. Time and place were no longer important to worship. Jesus himself had become my temple. Before him I bowed, in awe, to give thanks for life which is eternal because *I AM* gives meaning to being, to "is-ness," to each experience transcending hourly boundaries or a place in geography.

But, as I learn to worship at Jesus' feet, I discover also that his body—whenever it is found in time, wherever it is found in space—becomes my temple where love and grace and forgiveness reign and call forth my adoration and my praise. It is to this new temple, built and made glorious by the Spirit of Christ, that I with joy invite the wanderer from every nation to bend the knee with me and to give him praise for showing the path to exaltation; for incarnating the lesson of the way; for giving himself to show me that his is the way which leads to the glory of God-likeness—his image restored.

LITANY OF CONFESSION

A Litany of Confession

The litany of confession beginning on the next page is based on written responses from the audience attending sessions of the General Assembly of the Mennonite Church, held in June of 1977, Estes Park, Colorado. As a part of the Bible study experience in the Gospel of Mark, participants were invited to suggest areas of church and personal life where confession would be appropriate. The writer used these submissions to create the litany which follows.

Although the responses were not limited to the Markan frame of reference, a litany of confession nevertheless seems to be properly a part of the whole. No Spirit–directed insight into Mark's message is sterile. That insight inevitably leads to confession. Confession which grows out of involvement and learning changes a nondescript seed or an ugly bulb into a beautiful bloom. That beauty nods thanks and praise to the Maker above—a fitting act of worship.

This litany is not intended to be all–inclusive. Thoughtful readers may choose to substitute their own lines of contrition at certain places. Thus they will make the confession of sin and the supplication for grace and forgiveness uniquely their own.

A Litany of Confession

(During the entire litany one or more persons may pantomime various prayer postures: hands upraised open to implore; hands upraised closed—traditional; prostration on the ground in deep sorrow. Whether prostrate, kneeling, standing, or walking, each gesture of the persons pantomiming will reflect the emotional turmoil and spiritual desire of the supplicant. The supplicant may join in parts of the litany as directed.

There will be three LEADERS for this litany of confession. Each will have a complete script. LEADER A will lead the left one-third of the audience each time the first of the following responses is called for. LEADER B will lead the middle one-third of the audience each time the second of the following responses is called for. LEADER C will lead the right one-third of the audience in the third of the following responses . . .)

LEADER A—Oh Lord, hear our prayer!

LEADER B—Oh Lord, have mercy upon us!

LEADER C—Oh Lord, forgive us our sin!

*(A single narrator or Choric group may
speak all other material, as directed.)*

Religious they were
                    . . . as we
caught up in form
                    . . . as we
enslaved by tradition
                    . . . as we
without ears to hear
or eyes open to see
the shape of new kingdom truth—
            religious
            they were;
            oh, yes
no one could deny that;
            also
            bloodthirsty . . .
Oh Lord, have mercy upon us!
            . . . bloodthirsty
Oh Lord, have mercy upon us!
            . . . religious and bloodthirsty
Oh Lord, have mercy upon us!
            gentle
            pious
            people
            tempted oft
      to thirst for blood
            wherever
            Jesus

brings in his new wine
which
must have new wineskins
so that
old wineskins are laid aside . . .

Oh Lord, hear our prayer!
Oh Lord, forgive us our sin!
Oh Lord, have mercy upon us!

Sometimes . . .
Oh Lord, have mercy upon us!
the choice is between . . .
Oh Lord, have mercy upon us!
. . . sometimes
the choice is between
old wineskins and Jesus
Oh Lord, have mercy upon us!
. . . sometimes
we have chosen
old wineskins instead of Jesus
Oh Lord, forgive us our sin!
Oh Lord, hear our prayer!
—old wineskins instead of Jesus—
Oh Lord, have mercy upon us!

I confess, Father
I have not experienced deeply
the heart of Jesus
in his concern

for
—social justice
—for equality between all
          persons
—for the whole man
but too often
like the priest and Levite
—religious leaders
properly appointed and recognized—
too often
like the priest and Levite
I have walked by on the other side

Oh Lord, have mercy upon us!

I confess, Father
I have not been like a little child
—unpretentious
—humble
—unaspiring

but rather have denied
this model
for your kingdom . . .

. . too often I have been anxious
for position
for power
for achievement

Oh Lord, have mercy upon us!

I confess, Father
         I have become so dependent
                  on the comfortable home
                  of church structure
                  and familiar worship patterns
                  and old ways

         that
         I have resisted change
         and ignored
         the gentle nudgings of
         the Holy Spirit
                  —to respond
                  —to move
                  —to grow

. . . and thus have often missed
the new way
the kingdom way
on which Jesus walks

Oh Lord, have mercy upon us!

I confess, Father
         I have often been more concerned
                  with a precise interpretation
                  or a favorite dogma
                  or the success of a program

         than about people
                  —persons

> —hungry
> —hurting
> —needy
> —searching persons

> . . . like a Pharisee, Lord.

Too often, I've been like a Pharisee
> a Pharisee
> caught
> in a trap
> of his own making

Oh Lord, have mercy upon us!

> I confess, Father . . .
Oh Lord, have mercy upon us!
> I confess, Father . . .
>> so many
>> old wineskins
>> have become
>> idols
Oh Lord, forgive us our sin!
>> I have allowed
>> a just gratefulness
>> for my origins
>>> —and for my heritage—
>> to become an idol . . .

Oh Lord, forgive us our sin!
>> I have allowed

geography
and blood lines
and family names
and money
and color
to become idols . . .

Oh Lord, forgive us our sin!

. . . idols, Lord!
an unholy family of idols;
I have bowed down
before them all.

Oh Lord, hear our prayer!
Oh Lord, forgive us our sin!
Oh Lord, have mercy upon us!

. . . teach me, Father
to put away my idols
and worship
one God alone.

Oh Lord, hear our prayer!

I have brought with me offerings, Lord
—an offering
of contrition
—an offering
of repentance
—an offering
of new commitment:

> . . . my choice is
> to put away
> all of these false gods
> and worship at your feet

Oh Lord, hear our prayer!
Oh Lord, forgive us our sin!

> . . . my choice is
> to lay aside
> the old wineskins
> so the new wine
> of Jesus' kingdom
> will not be lost

Oh Lord, hear our prayer!
Oh Lord, forgive us our sin!

> . . . my choice is
> to turn from
> my wanderings
> to walk
> on the way
> with Christ

Oh Lord, hear our prayer!
Oh Lord, forgive us our sin!

> (. . . then will I hear

from heaven, and will
forgive their sin, and
will heal their land.)

Urie A. Bender is a free-lance writer living in Baden, Ontario. In addition to his years of service as an editor at Mennonite Publishing House, Scottdale, Pennsylvania, he has authored four books.

He has also written a number of historical pageants and plays, all of which have been produced. His first, *This Land Is Ours,* performed to sell-out houses at the Avon—one of the Stratford Shakespearean Theatres in Stratford, Ontario—in 1972 and again in 1973. (Also, in 1973, at Morris Civic Auditorium, South Bend, Indiana.) Another, *Tomorrow Has Roots* premiered at Century 2 Theatre in Wichita, Kansas, before the Tri-College Company took their production on the road for more than fifty performances in a number of states and provinces. A third, *In Search of a Country,* was produced in 1975 by Conrad Grebel College at the University of Waterloo, Waterloo, Ontario, to commemorate Anabaptist origins of the Mennonite Church.

Other productions have been completed for the Mennonite Brethren Church in California—produced by Pacific College and Mennonite Brethren Seminary; for the Church of the Brethren—produced by Elizabethtown College in Pennsylvania, for campus and General Conference performances; as well as for congregations and assemblies of the Mennonite Church.

In addition to writing, Bender has served as producer for one of his scripts, directed another, and acted in several. His commitment to the use of drama and other artistic forms within the Christian church has led him to a wide and supportive acquaintanceship among Mennonite artists, to brief teaching stints on various campuses in the field of creative writing, to Writer-in-Residence and Writing Fellow appointments, and to consistent efforts toward the raising of consciousness about artistic matters within several streams of the Mennonite Church.

This book of interpretations from the Gospel of Mark carries forward the author's concern for a new look at the biblical Christian message which can carry understandings beyond the clichés of traditional renderings of truth.

Urie and his wife, Dorothy, are the parents of two married daughters and have three grandchildren.